THIS IS
ANFIELD

THIS IS A CARLTON BOOK

Published in Great Britain in 2015 by
Carlton Books Limited
20 Mortimer Street
London W1T 3JW

Text and design © Carlton Books

A CIP catalogue for this book is available from the British Library

Project Editor: Matt Lowing
Editorial: Caroline Curtis and Chris Parker
Design: Russell Knowles and Darren Jordan
Production: Maria Petalidou
Index: Colin Hynson

ISBN: 978 1 78097 687 7

Printed in Dubai

10 9 8 7 6 5 4 3 2 1

Above: Rival captains Graeme Souness and Mark Higgins lead out
their respective teams for the Merseyside derby of November 1983.
Liverpool ran out 3-0 victors on this occasion but Anfield, once home
to Everton of course, has witnessed many titanic battles between the
Reds and Blues through the years.

Following pages: Liverpool prepare for action ahead of a fixture
in 2014/15. A colourful Kop, displaying the flags and banners which
contribute so richly to the Anfield atmosphere, provides the backdrop.

THIS IS
ANFIELD

The Official Illustrated History of
Liverpool FC's Legendary Stadium

MARK PLATT
WITH
WILLIAM HUGHES

CARLTON
BOOKS

Garuda Indonesia
WARRIOR
artered
LIVERPOOL FOOTBALL CLUB
EST · 1892
WALK ALONE
DALGLISH
#DEMAND
#DEMAND
LUCAS
21

CONTENTS

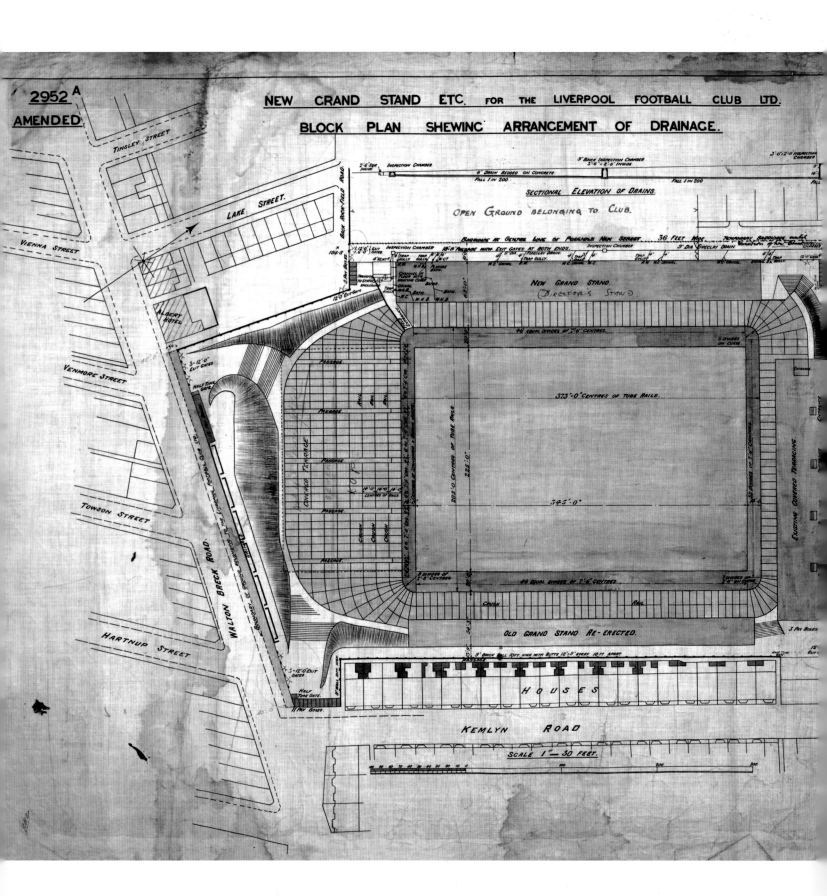

INTRODUCTION

Anfield. The name alone conjures up a million and one memories. Be they good, bad, tragic or triumphant.

It's a football ground like no other. Steeped in history and teeming with tradition; bursting at the seams with tales of famous games and legendary players.

One of the oldest and most iconic sporting arenas in the world, it was originally home to Everton Football Club but has long since become synonymous with Liverpool Football Club and the amazing success achieved by the Reds.

From humble origins it has gradually risen and now looms large over the surrounding rows of back-to-back terraced houses that have been there as long as the ground itself. The towering stands dominate the local skyline and it's become as much a symbol of the city as the Liver Buildings or St George's Hall.

Every other week thousands of supporters head towards the mecca that is Anfield and generations of Liverpudlians, especially in the last half a century, have been lucky enough to witness some of the most memorable and defining moments in football history ...

A swaying Kop singing along to songs by the Beatles in the mid-1960s and a portly policeman laughing out loud as the ecstasy of another title triumph erupts around him a couple of years later. Bill Shankly scolding a policeman for kicking a supporter's scarf into the dirt after the league title triumph of 1973, Davey Fairclough's leap of joy after flooring the flamboyant French champions

St Etienne on the way to conquering Europe for the first time in '77 and Terry McDermott's perm applying the finishing touch to a flowing move against Tottenham 12 months later, which Bob Paisley later described as the greatest Anfield goal he had ever seen.

John Barnes slaloming his way through the QPR defence in the late 1980s and the poignant images of flowers being laid on the pitch in memory of those who lost their lives at Hillsborough, back-to-back 4-3 thrillers in successive seasons against Newcastle during the 1990s and, in more recent times, Stevie G's "you beauty" moment when he burst the back of the net against Olympiacos to keep the Reds on course for Champions League glory in 2005.

Such memories, like countless others, are priceless. And they begin before a ball is even kicked. From the pungent smell of hot dogs and hamburgers to the cries of "hat, cap, scarf or a badge" on the walk up to the ground, a pre-match pint in one of the many local pubs, the heightened sense of anticipation as the turnstiles click and the excitement of buying a programme. Then there's the magical feeling you get when rising up the steps to catch that first glimpse of the green baize on which the action unfolds, the ear-splitting noise as the players enter the fray, the opening bars of "You'll Never Walk Alone", the roar of the crowd as the goals fly in or sporting applause if the result goes the other way.

The match-going experience may have changed considerably through the years but the sights, the sounds and the songs of Anfield are something to savour. Always have been and always will be. When it comes to watching football, it remains one of the truly great grounds.

In the annals of folklore, its place is forever assured and has been since as far back as 1892 when it was central to the split that saw Everton

Left: Plans drawn in April 1906 by renowned architect Archibald Leitch for the redevelopment of Anfield, including the huge terrace which would become known as the Kop.

Previous pages: A spectacular aerial view of Anfield in 2008. The landscape is to change significantly with work beginning on a stadium expansion in January 2015.

leave Anfield for Goodison and the subsequent formation of Liverpool, leading, of course, to the birth of a unique sporting rivalry.

Since then it has gone from strength to strength. Developing at a rapid rate as the new club on the Mersey began to flex its muscles in the fight for supremacy, both locally and nationally. Title triumphs, inspired by such esteemed greats as Alex Rasibeck, Elisha Scott and Billy Liddell, were celebrated and the crowds came in ever-increasing numbers. Then came the post-Shankly explosion and Anfield's reputation rocketed to a whole new level.

The legendary atmosphere, largely instigated by the inhabitants of the Spion Kop, is now widely renowned throughout football as being one of the

best and credited with being the inspiration for countless Liverpool victories. Such is the effect it can have on the opposition, it is often deemed worthy of a goal start.

The advent of European football has helped cultivate the legend further. Under the gaze of the floodlights the atmosphere somehow becomes even more electric, shaking the ground to its core and sending many opponents scurrying back to foreign shores. Inter Milan, Barcelona, Real Madrid and Bayern Munich, to name just a few, have all experienced it. How the mighty have fallen when faced with the intense wall of sound generated by a pumped-up Liverpool crowd.

It is such a fabled venue that all aspiring footballers, whether it be wearing the famous red

Above: Red nets, used from the 1960s to mid-1990s, were reintroduced ahead of the 2012/13 season at the request of new manager Brendan Rodgers. The first man to score in them? Fabio Borini.

shirt of Liverpool or running out for the opposition, dream of playing here at least once in their career.

For the supporters, Anfield means so much. As the great Bill Shankly once said: "The very word [Anfield] means more to me than I can describe." It's the spiritual home for so many. Hence the reason why the decision to stay and redevelop the ground, as opposed to the club building a new stadium on nearby Stanley Park, was met with universal approval.

What was once just a field on Anfield Road is now one of the most instantly recognizable plots of land in world football. It has undergone many changes through the years and the latest transformation will see its capacity rise to a figure just short of its record attendance that was set back in 1952.

It will provide Liverpool with a home befitting their status as one of the most famous football clubs on the planet and hopefully help keep them at the forefront of the game in this country and beyond.

As a new era now beckons and the redevelopment of the Main Stand comes to fruition, what better time to tell the Anfield story? It's one that has never before been told in such depth and in the pages that follow you'll learn all about the key figures, great games and significant moments that have made it what it is today.

Over 13 decades since it played host to its first football match, this is Anfield …

Mark Platt, 2015

THE EVERTON YEARS:
ANFIELD 1884–1892

CHAPTER ONE
THE EVERTON YEARS: ANFIELD 1884–1892

It's hard to imagine that Anfield, for so long synonymous with the triumphs and travails of Liverpool Football Club, was originally the home of Everton Football Club, their biggest and closest rivals.

To make sense of this you have to go way back to 1884, when association football in these parts was still in its infancy and playing second fiddle to rugby and rounders in the sporting stakes. Liverpool FC did not yet exist and the district of Anfield was a semi-rural settlement situated within the town of Walton-on-the-Hill.

Once known as Hangfield, due to the sloping nature of the terrain, Anfield had previously been an area of sparsely populated farmland. Only in the mid-1800s, when Liverpool's well-to-do shipping merchants and bankers started to move out of the city, did the landscape begin to change.

Along with the neighbouring districts of Everton and Breckfield, it suddenly became one of the more desirable places to live. Luxurious villas were built along the country lane that was Anfield Road, and from the rear of these properties were terrific views across the vast expanse of Stanley Park, which was opened amid much fanfare in 1870.

Eight years later, on a patch of land in this park, a team known as St Domingo's and then as Everton FC played its first games. In 1882 the club moved to nearby Priory Road but in the summer of 1884 was on the lookout for another new ground.

The best option was an undeveloped piece of land close by, owned by local brewers John and Joseph Orrell. Previously home to Everton Cricket Club, it was situated between Anfield Road and Walton Breck Road, directly opposite the home of Everton President John Houlding. An esteemed politician and publican, Houlding looked out on to this rather unkempt field every day. He could see that it had potential and so, through his

connections with the Orrells, he acquired it on the club's behalf.

Everton were allowed to lease the land in return for an annual fee of £100. With Houlding acting as the "representative tenant", his signature on the contract sealed the deal, the terms of which were: "That we, the Everton Football Club, keep the existing walls in good repair, pay the taxes, do not cause ourselves to be a nuisance to other tenants adjoining, and pay a donation each year to the Stanley Hospital in the name of Mr Orrell."

The location of the new ground was described in the local press as "a capital one" and, conveniently, it was just 200 yards from the Houlding-owned Sandon Hotel, which doubled up as the club's headquarters and team changing rooms. Around this time the surrounding

The Toss.

Burns on the rush.

J. Holt's little trick

Angus saves neatly.

Latta kicks the first goal for Everton

Everton pressing at the finish

EVERTON v. WEST BROMWICH ALBION AT LIVERPOOL.

area started to be built up into something that resembles what we see today, with the construction of terraced streets, small shops and pubs catering for the influx of new dwellers. Even though Anfield would not become part of Liverpool until 1895, the city was expanding at a rapid rate and the suburbs becoming more popular with the working classes. Previously it was just the wealthy who had enjoyed these parts.

Before the Anfield ground was in a state to stage football matches, though, there was a lot of work to be done. Large quantities of rubbish needed to be removed from what would become the pitch and the entire ground had to be enclosed. In the weeks leading up to the start of the 1884/85 season, club members set about getting it in shape; whether it was by offering their joinery skills or applying coats of paint to the new gates and hoardings, everybody chipped in.

Come 27 September 1884, the grounds were ready and history was made. As the doors of

Anfield were opened to the public for the first time, treasurer Charley Twemlow stood at the front gate with a bag to collect the entrance money. Everton captain William Parry then led his team on the short walk from the back of the Sandon to the new enclosure. Earlestown were the visitors and Everton coasted to a 5-0 win, Mick Higgins scoring the opening goal in front of an estimated 1,000 paying spectators.

Providing a further insight into what Anfield was like back then, author Thomas Keates tried to picture the scene. In his book about the early history of Everton Football Club, published during the 1928/29 season, he wrote: "A hoarding of boards was fixed on the walls, and rails around the playing pitch. Spectators stood on the intervening sods, a very humble stand crouching on the east for officials, members, pressmen and affluents."

Over the course of the next 18 months, some major changes were implemented. The stand,

Above: A representation of Everton's home game against West Brom at Anfield in October 1890 as portrayed by the *Illustrated Sporting and Dramatic News*. The Baggies won 3-2.

which consisted of ten tiered rows of wooden benches, was moved to the opposite side, currently the site of the Main Stand. In its place a new, and much grander, covered pavilion was built by local tradesman George Rutherford. It cost £64 and ran almost the full length of the pitch, while towards the corner of Kemlyn Road and Walton Breck Road a stilted press box was erected.

In 1885, though, the land upon which Everton were playing was put up for sale by Joseph Orrell. To save the club from having to up sticks for a third time, Houlding dug deep into his own pockets and met the asking price to purchase Anfield outright, meaning that he was now the club's landlord as well as President. Given that football's increasing popularity in the Victorian era was clearly evident at Anfield, this seemed a sound investment.

When FA Cup holders Blackburn came to play a friendly in September 1885, a then record crowd of 3,500 squeezed into the enclosure. Supporters were reported to be "packed tightly around the playing area" and so to accommodate demand further improvement to the ground took place.

Ahead of the 1886/87 season, work was completed on the first ever stand at the south side, or what we now know as the Kop end. Originally called the Oakfield Road stand or bank, it was a simple bank of wooden terracing, built on top of a cinder mound, behind which was a muddy patch of land, triangular in shape, where the visiting circus had often pitched their tent. It cost £1,500 to erect and was capable of accommodating 4,000 spectators. The following year a larger version was erected at the Anfield Road end.

With more and more high-profile friendlies being arranged, the increased capacity was certainly needed. In April 1887 for example, FA Cup holders Aston Villa paid their first visit to Anfield. It attracted an impressive crowd of 8,000 but, according to the *Liverpool Courier*, there was room for improvement. "The arrangements for such a huge crowd were altogether inadequate for not only are the barriers frail in the extreme, but also the available standing space, on the entrance side, is so small that the people crowded so close to the field that only with great difficulty could kicks from the corner be taken. Moving about was out of the question as the assemblage formed one compact mass."

Six weeks later, another prestigious fixture was played, this time against the soon to be "Invincibles" of Preston North End. For the first time in Anfield history the attendance reached 10,000. This was great for the club's finances but not such a fruitful afternoon for the team, who suffered a heavy loss. Still, it was because of games like this that word quickly spread about the impressive Everton ground.

In February 1888 it was awarded the honour of staging its first FA Cup semi-final, chosen as the neutral venue for the tie between Preston North End and Crewe Alexandra. This was a huge occasion for the club but one that was ultimately ruined by the weather. A light falling of snow the night before settled on the pitch and when the sun came out the following morning it melted, turning the playing surface into what was best described as a "dismal swamp". Preston adapted better to the slushy conditions and, kicking into the Anfield

Road end, they quickly racked up a 5-0 lead, from which there was no return for Crewe.

The Railwaymen later lodged an appeal, claiming the pitch was unsatisfactory, and demanding the game be replayed. Ultimately this was to no avail and Anfield's reputation remained intact. So much so that the following year it was again recognized by the Football Association, who deemed it good enough to host England's Home International match with Ireland (see page 19).

By this point in history, Everton had become founder members of the Football League and on the first day of fixtures in this new competition, Anfield was able to boast the biggest crowd when 10,000 witnessed the hosts' 2-1 victory over Accrington. Merseyside was now widely considered to be the hottest bed of football fanaticism in the country. Everton were firmly established as one of the leading clubs and they had a ground equipped to match the progress of the team.

In January 1890 Anfield even trialled the use of floodlights for a game against Sheffield United. "16 Wells Patent Lights were erected 25 feet [7.6 metres] above the Anfield ground and the match ball was painted white so it could be more easily picked out in the ghostly glow," reported the local press. This was a novel idea and one that attracted 8,000 spectators.

With the capacity now extended to around 20,000, the *Football Field* magazine provided the following appraisal: "The enclosure now bears the resemblance of a huge circus, with its two immense galleries, rising tier above tier, and its covered stands stretching the length of the ground on one side, and for the greater part of that distance on the other. Every inch of available space was utilized, and the spectacle was of a most imposing description."

It was just as well Anfield had been expanded because in 1890 the dockworkers of the city won the right to have their working week cut from six days to five-and-a-half. That meant their Saturday afternoons were now free, enabling them to enjoy the increasingly popular pastime of going to see the match. As a result, attendances rose once again.

Also around this time a distinctive new feature was added to the Anfield landscape: a flagpole 15.25 metres (50 feet) tall, which had once been the top mast of Isambard Kingdom Brunel's famous ship the SS *Great Eastern*. It had been purchased by the club from a shipyard in Rock Ferry, floated across the Mersey and hauled up to Anfield by a team of horses. It was positioned at the corner of the ground where Walton Breck Road meets Kemlyn Road and has remained there ever since.

From this new flagpole flew Anfield's first championship pennant in 1891. After finishing runners-up the previous season, Everton, at only the third attempt, topped the First Division table with a team captained by the great Andrew Hannah. Everything about the club seemed to be on the up, but trouble was brewing behind the scenes and Everton's association with Anfield would soon meet an acrimonious end.

The following season was to be the team's last at the ground. A bitter dispute erupted when Houlding, as the club's landlord, increased the rental charge on Anfield. The majority of members on the Everton committee were incensed and the fall-out was an almighty one. It ended with them eventually upping sticks to a new ground on the other side of Stanley Park.

From its humble origins, Everton had transformed Anfield into one of the finest football grounds of the Victorian era, but as the departing Evertonians were only too quick to crow, "What use is that if there's no team to play in it?"

After just eight years in existence Anfield faced an uncertain future.

GREAT GAME:
England v Ireland, British Championship
2 March 1889

The rise of Anfield was a rapid one. Within less than five years it went from being an unsightly piece of wasteland to a football ground deemed good enough to stage international football.

Being selected to host England's Home International clash with Ireland in March 1889 was a huge honour for Everton Football Club and its members, who had developed the ground from scratch in such a short space of time.

It was only the second time that the national team had played in the city. Although no Everton players featured for either England or Ireland on the day, there was still plenty of interest among the local football fans and a crowd of around 6,000 were in attendance to witness this historic occasion.

Poor fixture scheduling meant the game was played on the same afternoon as the quarter-finals of the FA Cup, so with a lot of players opting to play for club rather than country, England's team was a severely weakened one. Nine of the 11 won their first caps at Anfield, including captain John Brodie of Wolves.

Ireland took an early lead thanks to a header from James Wilton. However, England proved far too strong, despite all the new faces, and eventually ran out the comfortable 6-1 winners, with Burnley's Jack Yates scoring a hat trick on his one and only international appearance.

Right: Produced for Anfield's first international in March 1889, this is believed to be the earliest England home programme offered at auction and also features Everton's fixtures for the 1888/1889 season.

ANFIELD LEGEND
JOHN HOULDING

The most significant figure in the early history of both Everton and Liverpool Football Clubs is John Houlding. Without him, football might never have been played at Anfield.

Born and bred in the city, Houlding was a highly esteemed, self-made, local businessman and Conservative politician, who later rose to the position of Lord Mayor. Educated at Liverpool College, he had worked from the age of 11 and eventually set up his own successful brewery.

An active Orangeman and sports enthusiast, Houlding was a prominent figure in the city and viewed as the natural choice when appointed Everton Football Club's first President. The back of his house on Anfield Road overlooked the pitch on Stanley Park where the team originally played, while the nearby Sandon pub, one of a string that he owned, was also utilized as the club's headquarters. It was Houlding who arranged for Everton to rent the field opposite his home, which became Anfield, and in 1885 he purchased the land himself.

He helped establish Everton as one of the leading clubs of this time and developed Anfield into a ground widely considered to be among the best in the country. The acrimonious split of 1892 left him with a first-class enclosure but no team to play in it. Rather than give up on football, he decided to form a new club and ploughed more of his own personal fortune into making it a success. Liverpool FC was born – and the rest is history.

As Chairman for the first four years and President until his death in 1902, he saw the club make rapid strides – gaining election to the Football League in 1893 and becoming champions just eight years later. Much greater success lay on the horizon for both clubs on Merseyside, but "King John" had laid the foundations for everything that followed.

> "*Everton Football Club's fame was largely due to his energy and organising ability, and after the differences which resulted in the removal of the club ground to Goodison Park, he established the Liverpool Club.*"
> **Liverpool Mercury, 18 March 1902**

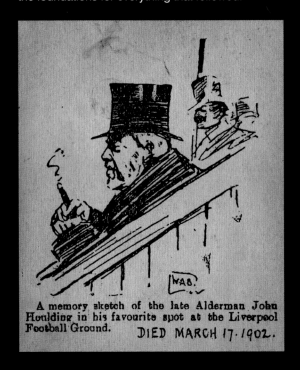

A memory sketch of the late Alderman John Houlding in his favourite spot at the Liverpool Football Ground. DIED MARCH 17. 1902.

Left: This sketch of "King John" watching a game from his seat at Anfield, was published in the local press along with his obituary following his death in 1902.

Right: An official portrait painted by prominent artist George Hall Neale in 1898 soon after John Houlding had been appointed Lord Mayor of Liverpool.

THE REDS ARE COMING UP THE HILL: ANFIELD 1892–1928

CROWD
SPION KOP
L'POOL

CHAPTER TWO

THE REDS ARE COMING UP THE HILL: ANFIELD 1892–1928

Fears that the bitter split would leave Anfield "a howling wilderness" were unfounded. Faced with the prospect of being the landlord of a ground with no team to play in it, John Houlding proceeded to form a new club. Liverpool Football Club came into existence during the summer of 1892 and one of sports great rivalries was born.

When the dust eventually settled after what had been a tumultuous few months in the city, Anfield prepared itself for the dawn of a new era. In an open letter to *Field Sport*, Liverpool secretary William Barclay wrote that, "the ground is in better order now than it has ever been before at this stage of the year".

Visually, nothing much was altered, but the new club did acquire the use of 27 Kemlyn Road, which backed on to the players' entrance at Anfield. This was to be used as the new changing

rooms, thus ending the tradition of players having to walk from the Sandon and through the crowds of supporters before and after each game.

The furore caused by Everton's move to Goodison stoked up the interest in football on Merseyside, and Liverpool's first open training session at Anfield was witnessed by a crowd of 6,000. Having had their initial application to compete alongside Everton in the Football League rejected, the team began life in the Lancashire League and just a few weeks later warmed up with a friendly at home to Rotherham Town.

"No better game will be witnessed on any of the plots in the neighbourhood," was the defiant boast of the Liverpool directors. But while that may well have been the case, the crowd at Anfield, estimated to be in the region of just a few hundred

Previous pages: FA Cup action against Gillingham in January 1914. Liverpool won 2-0 thanks to late goals from Bill Lacey and Bob Ferguson.

Left: The massed ranks of supporters on the Kop cheer on the Reds during a match in 1914.

Right: The first Liverpool team picture from 1892. It includes Jock Smith, second from left on the front row, who sored the club's first league goal against Higher Walton.

J. McQue.   J McCartney.   A. Hannah.   S. H. Ross.   M. McQueen.   D. McLean.   J. McBride   A. Dick (*Trainer*).
T. Wyllie.   J. Smith.   J. Miller.   M. McVean.   H. McQueen.

at best, was dwarfed by the 10,000 who chose to watch their football at Goodison that afternoon.

Nevertheless, it was an encouraging start for Houlding and his new team of "Anfielders". The President kicked off Liverpool's inaugural match and then watched as they romped to a 7-1 victory. The honour of scoring the club's first goal went to Tom Miller, while Tom Wylie was a hat-trick hero.

A successful first season followed and the fledgling "Livers" were on the rise. In February 1894 a memorable FA Cup victory over Preston North End attracted a new record Anfield attendance of 18,000.With the prospect of even bigger crowds once promotion to the First Division had been secured, a new 3,000-capacity grandstand was built that summer. Measuring 100 metres (360 feet) long and containing 11 rows of seats, plus a balcony at the back, it was described as a "handsome and commodious building" and believed to be "probably the most imposing football erection in existence".

The club's long-term future at Anfield, however, was often the subject of speculation during these formative years. On more than one occasion there was talk in the press that they might be forced to look for a new ground, the *Football Echo* even going as far as to report that "prospecting has already taken place", in the south end of the city. The sticking point centred around plans to purchase an extra piece of land that would allow them to extend the playing surface. When negotiations broke down in 1897, the *Athletic News* revealed that a site "on the Old Swan tramline" was being lined up, but three weeks later the matter was amicably resolved.

That same year, the Anfield Road end was covered and it would have also been around this time that the ground first echoed to the now familiar battle cry of "Come on you Reds" after the colour of the team's shirts had been switched

from blue and white. The Anfield turnstiles were now clicking faster than ever before, and while Everton may still have been proving to be the bigger draw among the football enthusiasts of Merseyside, the younger of the city's two clubs was gaining in popularity all the time.

This was in no small part down to the success on the pitch. Under the leadership of secretary Tom Watson, Liverpool firmly established themselves as one of the country's top teams. They reached the FA Cup semi-final in 1897 and then again two years later, when they also finished runners-up in the league.

In 1901 Anfield was home to the champions of England for a second time as Alex Raisbeck captained the Reds to the first of their 18 First Division titles. On the back of this success a new Anfield Road enclosure was built in 1903, a year after the club's founding father John Houlding had passed away. The ground Houlding built had served Liverpool well, but the club had made such rapid strides that it was in danger of outgrowing its home.

The official capacity was now believed to be between 28,000 and 30,000, but on Good Friday 1906 the need for that to be increased was never more alarmingly evident. Everton were the visitors to Anfield, and interest in the game was huge. It was to be a vintage season for the city's two clubs; Liverpool chasing the league and Everton the FA Cup. And the inclement spring weather, coupled with the bank holiday, meant that the locals turned out in record numbers.

According to the *Liverpool Courier*, 35,000 somehow crammed inside, while thousands more were locked out. It was reported that "all round the playing pitch enthusiastic supporters of either club swarmed around the touch line. Others climbed on the roofs of the stands while several partisans

> ## "... all round the playing pitch enthusiastic supporters of either club swarmed around the touch line. Others climbed on the roofs of the stands while several partisans swarmed up the pillars supporting the roofs and perched themselves in forks of the ironworks."
>
> ### Liverpool Courier

swarmed up the pillars supporting the roofs and perched themselves in forks of the ironworks."

The game had to be stopped several times due to fans encroaching on to the pitch as a result of the severe overcrowding and "at one time it was feared that the game might have to be abandoned". Amazingly there were no reported injuries, but it was clear for all to see that expansion of the ground was required.

Despite a 1-1 draw that day Liverpool went on to clinch their second League Championship, and soon the club would have a home befitting such an illustrious team. Immediately after the final curtain came down on the 1905/06 season, the builders moved in and for the next three months Anfield resembled a construction site. The man entrusted with the task of overseeing the ground's redevelopment was the highly esteemed Glasgow-based engineer Archibald Leitch (see page 42).

This was an extremely ambitious project, arguably the largest ever undertaken in Anfield history. To complete the work in such a short timescale was a huge task, and it was to prove a lot more arduous than expected. But during the summer of 1906 everybody chipped in, even Tom Watson and the directors, who all took great pride in what was taking shape.

As the next campaign approached, there was much excitement surrounding the "new Anfield". Before the opening home game, selected journalists were invited to take a sneak preview and the *Liverpool Echo*

commented that, "the entire scheme is modelled on a new departure from what football grounds are generally supposed to be."

Anfield was now completely walled in and its "fancy brick settings" gave it a striking new look from the outside. The number of turnstiles rose from 26 to 47 and large exit gates were put in place. The pitch was raised by 1.5 metres (5 feet) and slightly repositioned, while the corners of the ground were rounded to avoid wasting any space and a narrow paddock ensured that all four stands were now joined, allowing supporters on the terraces to switch ends depending on which way Liverpool were shooting.

The old Main Stand was carefully dismantled and rebuilt on the opposite side to replace the structure on Kemlyn Road. In its place, a new grandstand was erected and this, when fully completed the following season, became the first stand in football to be made using reinforced concrete, by a method known as the "Hennebique System". Its iron-framed barrel roof also featured a distinctive red and white, mock-Tudor-style, arched gable in the centre. This was a Leitch trademark and would come to symbolize the ground for more than 60 years.

What was to become more famous, though, was the elevated terrace to its right. Now extended and consisting of 132 tiered steps, it towered over the rest of the ground and could house up to 20,000 spectators. It would soon become universally known as the Spion Kop, after a hill now in modern-day South Africa, which was the scene of a significant

Right: A pin badge of the 1907 Liverpool team that was the subject of one of the first known supporter songs at Anfield "Hurrah for the Reds".

battle during the Boer War six years earlier, during which many soldiers from Liverpool were killed.

Local lore has always maintained that Anfield's large, open terrace was christened the Spion Kop by Ernest "Bee" Edwards, then sports editor of the *Liverpool Echo*. However, no evidence has ever emerged to support this claim. The more credible explanation is that it was the supporters, many of whom had fought in the war, who first referred to it as such.

We do know that Bee picked up on this and encouraged further use of this description because he later wrote in his newspaper column, "This huge wall of earth has been termed 'Spion Kop' and no doubt this apt name will always be used in future in referring to this spot."

It is unfeasible to assume that all supporters immediately started calling it by that name, and only after 1912 is it consistently referenced in press reports as "the Kop". At what point the club adopted it is also open to conjecture, there being no tangible proof of the term being used "officially" until a later redevelopment in 1928. But even though Liverpool's wasn't the first Spion Kop in English football – that distinction goes to Woolwich Arsenal in 1904 – it certainly became the most well-known.

Within a month of the revamped Anfield opening its gates for the first time, a new record crowd of 40,000 was in attendance to witness the always eagerly anticipated Merseyside derby. Unlike the previous meeting, it passed off without incident. The aim of the directors was "to provide as compact and comfortable a ground as possible in which every person no matter what position will have a full view of the game", and these major refurbishments attracted admiring glances from other clubs – not least near neighbours Everton, who swiftly followed suit by engaging the services of Leitch to design a new stand at Goodison.

Anfield was now widely considered to be one of the "finest and most up-to-date grounds in the country". In 1908 it was chosen to host the FA Cup semi-final

Left: A family photograph of Tom Watson, the man who guided Liverpool to their first two league titles after enjoying previous success at Sunderland.

between Newcastle United and Fulham, a game that ended in a landslide 6-0 victory for the Geordies over their then non-league opponents.

For the best part of the next two decades Anfield's appearance changed very little, and then in March 1921 it was given the Royal seal of approval. King George V and Queen Mary, who had stayed over in the city after attending the Grand National at Aintree the previous afternoon, were the guests of honour at another FA Cup semi-final clash – this time between Wolverhampton Wanderers and Cardiff City.

The following year, Liverpool's directors decided to invest in the future by opening a designated area of the ground just for juveniles. Occupying terrace space at the Anfield Road end of the Kemlyn Paddock, it ran half the length of the pitch and could hold 4,000. Known as the Boys' Pen, it was to become a rite of passage for all aspiring Liverpudlians and a cherished part of Anfield folklore.

It was also around this time that a possible new three-tiered stand at the Anfield Road end was first spoken about. But while the revolutionary concept of the so-called "hat-trick stand" got no further than the planning stage, a significant redevelopment of the ground was soon to take place and Anfield would never be the same again.

GREAT GAME
Liverpool v Everton, First Division
17 November 1894

Everton's much-awaited first return to their former home was a game that captured the imagination of everyone in the city. Just two years after the bitter split they made the short journey back across Stanley Park as Anfield staged its first Liverpool–Everton derby.

The rivalry between the two clubs may have still been in its infancy, but it was already an intense one – according to the *Liverpool Mercury* the locals were "roused to a pitch of unusual excitement". A month earlier the inaugural League meeting between them had resulted in a 3-0 victory for Everton at Goodison. Liverpool were hell-bent on revenge, but the formbook suggested otherwise. While the Toffeemen topped the table, the hosts languished near the foot, second to bottom with just one win in 14 games to their name.

Such was the interest in the game that, in the hours leading up to kick-off, all roads around the ground were reported to be much busier than on a normal match day. Although "extra accommodation had been provided" for the expected large crowd, it was quickly filled and Anfield was "packed to the utmost" for this historic meeting. The crowd, which eventually numbered 30,000, was a new record for the ground and the spectators were treated to a thrilling spectacle.

First blood went to the visitors when Bob Kelso scored from the penalty spot after half an hour. David Hannah levelled matters 10 minutes into the second half. Then a breathtaking end to the game saw Everton's Alex Latta score what looked to be the winner five minutes from time, only for Jimmy Ross to then rescue a point with a last-gasp spot kick.

On reflection it was agreed that a draw was a fair result, although the local press were keen to highlight what had been "a most creditable performance on the part of the younger organization".

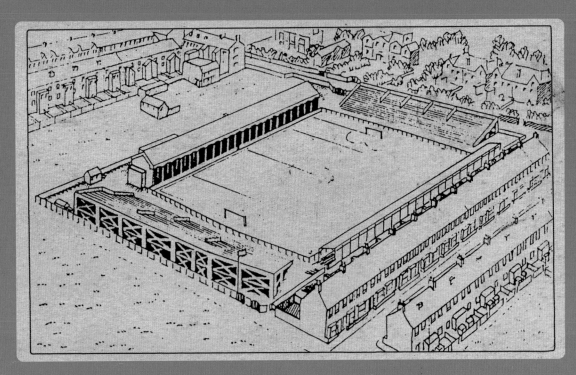

Right: An artist's impression of how the Anfield stadium and surrounding area would have looked in 1894.

Liverpool *Football Ground*

Above: An animation from a local paper with the female figure of Victory crowning Liverpool's captain as a Liver Bird looks on after the Reds won Division One in 1901.

Right: Supporters milling about early outside Anfield on a match day, circa 1910–12. They are pictured on the corner of Walton Breck Road and Kemlyn Road, now better known as flagpole corner.

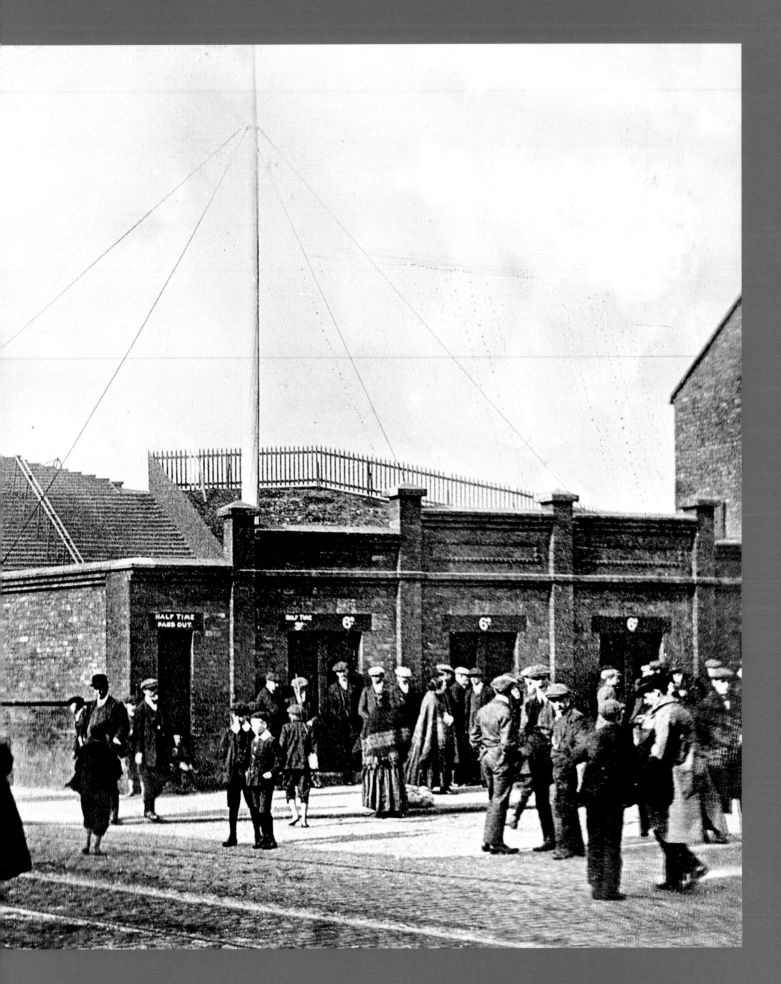

Text visible in image: HALF TIME PASS OUT, HALF TIME 3d, 6d, 6d, 6d

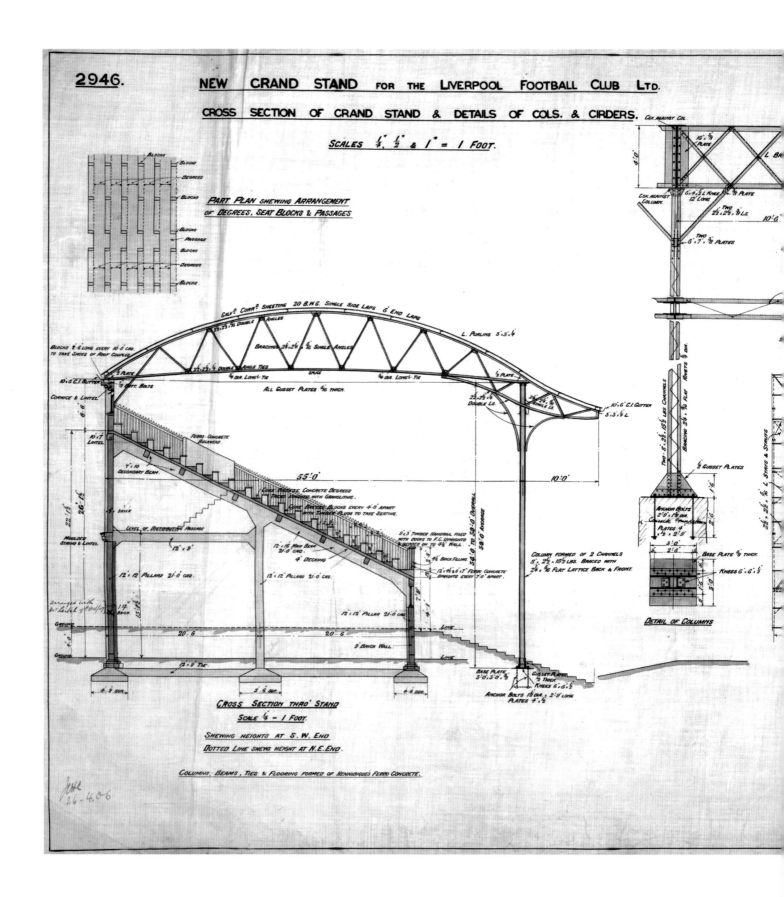

2946.

NEW GRAND STAND FOR THE LIVERPOOL FOOTBALL CLUB LTD.

CROSS SECTION OF GRAND STAND & DETAILS OF COLS. & GIRDERS.

SCALES ¼", ½" & 1" = 1 FOOT.

PART PLAN SHEWING ARRANGEMENT
OF DEGREES, SEAT BLOCKS & PASSAGES

CROSS SECTION THRO' STAND

SCALE ¼" = 1 FOOT.

SHEWING HEIGHTS AT S.W. END
DOTTED LINE SHEWS HEIGHT AT N.E. END.

COLUMNS, BEAMS, TIES & FLOORING FORMED OF HENNIQUE'S FERRO CONCRETE.

DETAIL OF COLUMNS

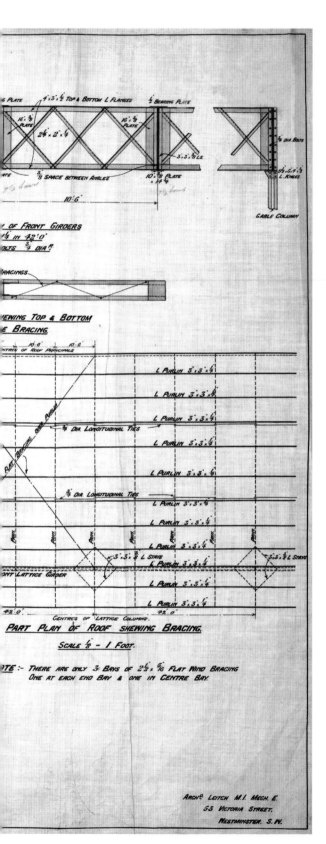

Left: More of Archibald Leitch's drawings for the proposed new "Grand Stand" – or Lake Street/Main Stand at Anfield, which would be a pioneering structure.

Below: A painted wooden sign that was removed from the Kop during reroofing work in the mid-1960s. It is thought to have dated from 1928 or even 1906.

Bottom: A photograph published in *The Builder* in 1906, showing the new Main Stand at Anfield, which was one of the first constructed using the Hennebique Ferro Reinforced Concrete method.

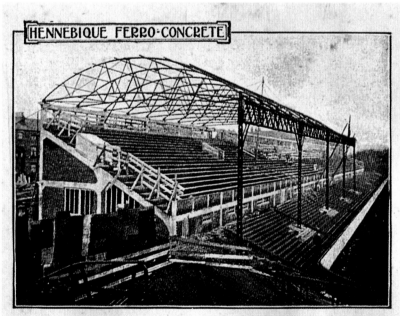

Football Grand Stand, Liverpool.
Built for THE LIVERPOOL FOOTBALL CLUB.
Engineer: ARCHIBALD LEITCH, M.I.Mech.E.

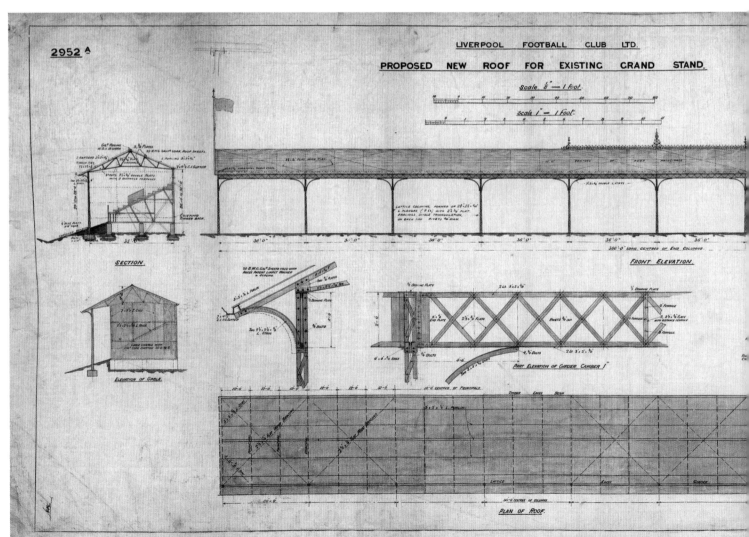

Opposite top: Liverpool's squad pose at the back of the Main Stand for an official photograph ahead of the 1908/09 season. It also features trainers Bill Connell and George Fleming.

Below: When Archibald Leitch set about redeveloping the ground in 1906 he drew up plans to resite the original Main Stand, complete with a new roof, on Kemlyn Road, where it was to remain until 1963.

Below right: Ephraim Longworth executes his famous "overhead glide" – a high bicycle-style kick. Longworth played 490 games for LFC between 1910 and 1928 before taking up a coaching role at Anfield.

> " [the aim is to] provide as compact and comfortable a ground as possible in which every person no matter what position will have a full view of the game."
> **Liverpool Football Club**

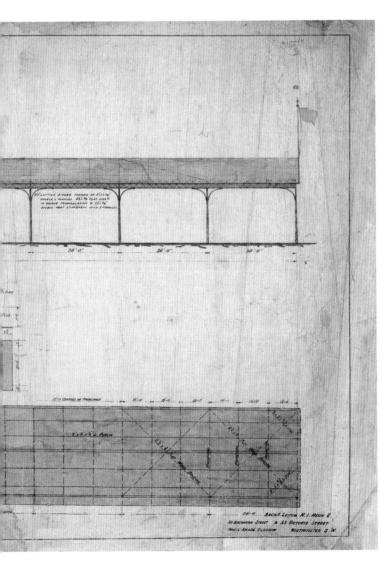

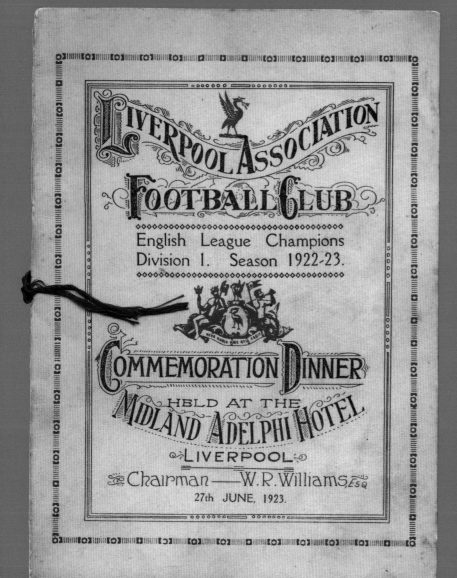

Above: Liverpool's league champions of 1921–22. Managed by David Ashworth the team featured the likes of Elisha Scott, Ephraim Longworth, Donald Mackinlay and Harry Chambers.

Left: The programme for the 1923 celebration dinner held at the Adelphi Hotel to toast Liverpool's fourth top-flight title success.

Opposite top: Seven Liverpool players, including original hard man Walter Wadsworth, line up behind manager David Ashworth on the junction of the Main Stand (left) and Anfield Road terrace.

Right: Supporters soak up the pre-match atmosphere on the uncovered Kop. Note that the "Liverpool Football Club" sign is yet to be added to the famous arched gable centerpiece of Main Stand.

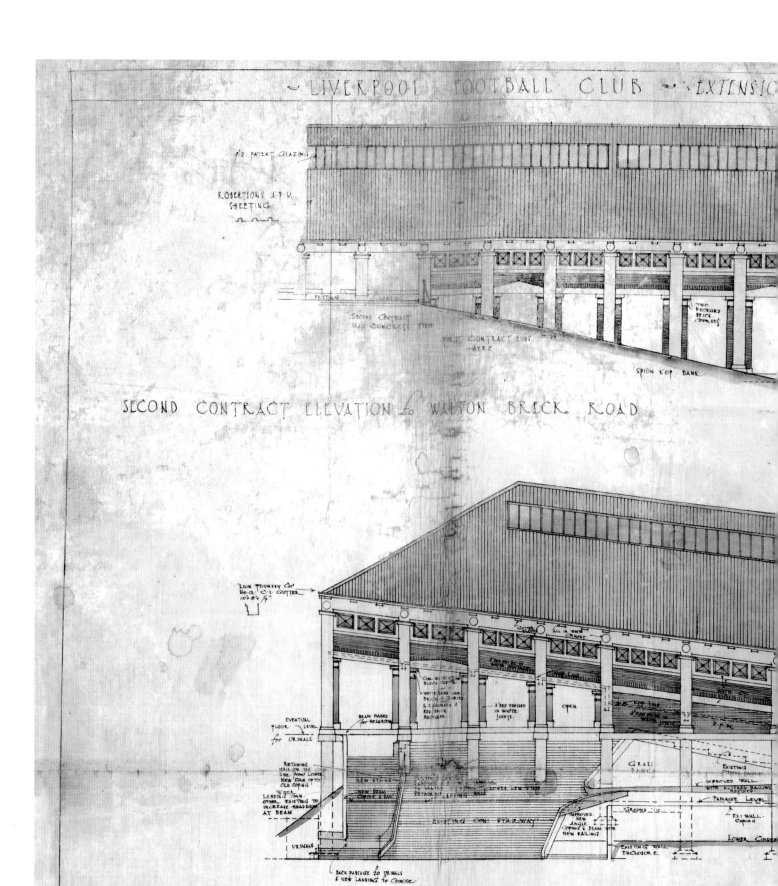

~ LIVERPOOL FOOTBALL CLUB ~ EXTENSIO

SECOND CONTRACT ELEVATION to WALTON BRECK ROAD

SECOND CONTRACT ELEVATION to KEMLYN ROAD.

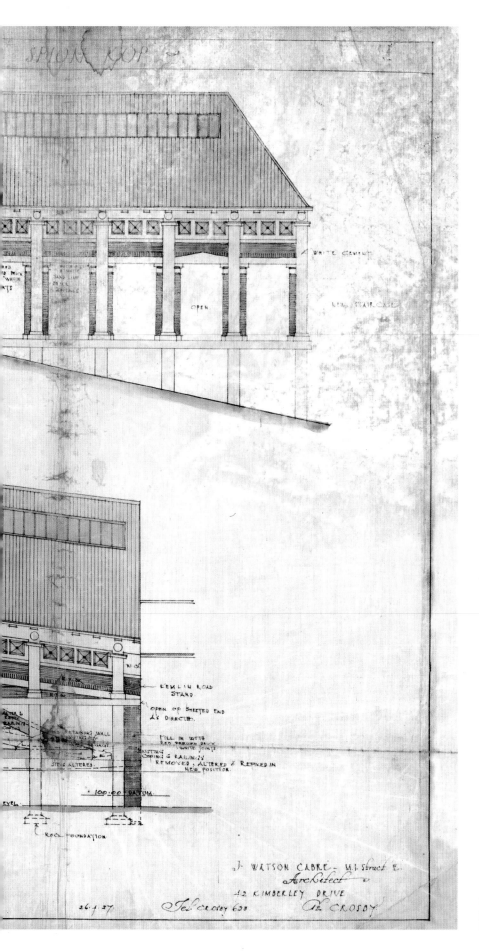

"*This huge wall of earth has been termed 'Spion Kop' and no doubt this apt name will always be used in future in referring to this spot.*"

Ernest "Bee" Edwards

Left: Architect's drawings from May 1927 depicting the proposed elevations for the new roof of the Spion Kop. Work was completed the following year.

ANFIELD LEGEND
ARCHIBALD LEITCH

If any one person can be credited with totally transforming the look and feel of Anfield in the early part of the last century, it is Archibald Leitch. Between 1899 and 1939, the Scottish architect was commissioned to work on more than 20 football stadiums across Britain.

Born in Glasgow in 1865, Leitch initially trained as a consulting engineer and factory architect. His first foray into football came with Rangers, the club he had supported as a boy and, despite being implicated in the Ibrox disaster of 1902, he quickly became a leading expert in this field.

He was hired by Liverpool in 1906, shortly after the club's second league title triumph. Anfield had changed very little since the days when Everton had been tenants and the directors decided it was time for a revolutionary redesign. Leitch, who also later lived on Merseyside for a short while, duly delivered.

He changed the appearance of the ground almost entirely, with the standout new additions being a Main Stand that featured his trademark gable roof and a huge bank of uncovered terracing that would soon become known as the Spion Kop. As a finishing touch, large exit gates on each side and a smart new perimeter wall were also erected, making Anfield one of the finest grounds in the land, the benefits of which were to be enjoyed by generations of Liverpudlians.

Other notable grounds that profited from the work of Leitch included Goodison Park, Old Trafford, Highbury, Villa Park, Stamford Bridge and Hampden. While the majority of the stands he built, including those at Anfield, have now long since been demolished, they certainly stood the test of time and left a legacy.

Left: Archibald Leitch was a pioneering figure in British football ground design and also worked on developments at Celtic, Rangers, Everton and Hampden Park.

Right: Sketches of Leitch's plans for the gable on the Main Stand at Anfield and, above, the finished design, complete with the "Liverpool Football Club" sign, which was added many years after the stand was first built.

"The entire scheme is modelled on a new departure from what football grounds are generally supposed to be."

***Liverpool Echo* on Archibald Leitch's Anfield design**

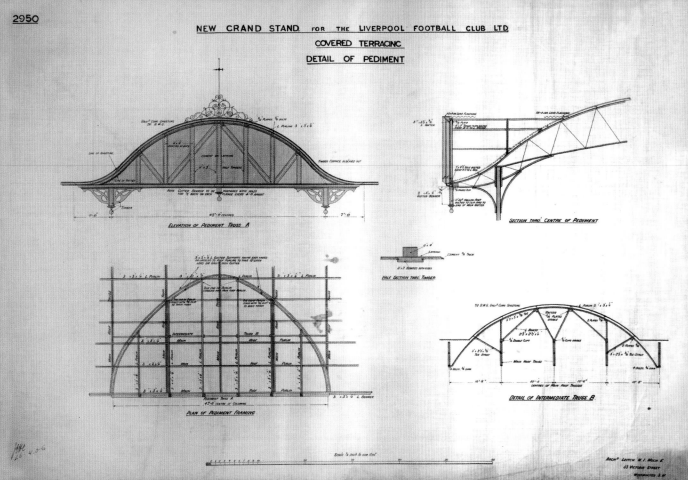

YOU'LL NEVER WALK ALONE: THE FANS

CHAPTER THREE

YOU'LL NEVER WALK ALONE: THE FANS

"We are the famous, the famous Kopites." Those are the words of a popular refrain that couldn't be more true. When it comes to support, Anfield can genuinely claim to have been blessed with the best. Universally known as the "Twelfth Man", the Liverpool crowd is renowned for sticking by the team through thick and thin. It is an ethos that has earned the club legions more followers around the world.

It's on match days that a football ground comes alive. The players may provide the entertainment but without the backdrop of supporters the spectacle is far less appealing. As the late, great, Celtic and Scotland manager Jock Stein said: "Football without fans is nothing."

On countless occasions down the years Liverpool's extra man has roared the Reds on to victory from seemingly impossible situations. There

was no greater advocate of their backing than Bill Shankly. "I would have to invent another word to fully describe the Anfield spectators," he once said. "It is more than fanaticism, it's a religion. To the many thousands who come here to worship, Anfield isn't a football ground, it's a sort of shrine. These people are not simply fans, they're more like members of one extended family."

The passion of the "Liverpool family" can be traced right back to the club's formative years when the first supporters were charged 4d for the privilege of watching the "Team of all the Macs". Without the staunch backing of those Victorian Liverpudlians the club may not have survived. Only 300 witnessed Liverpool's first competitive game in September 1892 but attendances steadily rose. There was an abundance of skilled workers and

Previous pages: Flags, banners and scarves on the Kop as fans cheer on the team during a 3-2 win over West Ham United in August 1972.

Left: A giant Liver Bird flag is waved on the Kop in August 2005. It also features five stars, denoting each of the club's European Cup triumphs.

Right: Steven Gerrard says farewell following his final game at Anfield in May 2015. The Kop had displayed a pre-match mosaic in his honour.

clerks employed in the Anfield and Breckfield communities and their jobs came with the added perk of half-day working on Saturdays. This facilitated a trip to the football in the afternoon and Liverpool were soon one of the best-supported teams in the country.

The match-going culture was a lot different back then. Whereas the Reds now boast a truly global fanbase, as late as the 1960s the majority lived within walking distance of Anfield. Before cars became an affordable mode of transport, most would travel to Anfield on foot or bicycle, parking up in the back-yards of surrounding terraced houses. For those arriving from further afield, trams stopped near both ends of the ground – even star players such as Tommy Lawrence and Roger Hunt were regular passengers.

While the working classes gathered on the terraces behind either goal, the so-called "toffs" would take up their positions in the stands. Yet no matter what their vantage point, they all had a common goal: to support Liverpool Football Club.

In an attempt to delve into the psyche of Reds supporters, *Echo* journalist Ernest "Bee" Edwards ventured on to the Kop in the 1920s. He was surprised by what he discovered, writing: "...the Kop is the home of the loyalists. I had expected slashing attacks on players but found praise and kindness. The kind way they talked of the players astonished me. Anfield's all right if it can keep this man at their back."

Down the years so many great Liverpudlians have passed through the turnstiles that, among a cast of thousands, it is almost impossible to single out individuals. Certain characters, however, will always be remembered.

Jimmy Phillips became the self-proclaimed team mascot in the 1930s, running on to the pitch to shake the hand of each player prior to kick-off. Three decades later a supporter known as Johnny Walker would regularly emerge from the Kop before the teams came out and kept the crowd entertained with a humorous repertoire of on-field antics, such as pretending to score with an imaginary ball. Then there was Dr Fun, aka Lenny Campbell from Huyton, who attended games during the 1980s and 1990s dressed head-to-toe in red (including a fetching top hat) while carrying a hand puppet called Charlie! There were no gimmicks as far as Bobby Wilcox was concerned. A big-hearted Liverpudlian, he was an Anfield regular from an early age and travelled all over Europe to watch the Reds in action, always preaching the virtues of supporting the team through ups and downs. Much-loved and highly respected by all who met him, such was the esteem in which he was held by friends, fellow fans and, indeed, the club, that flags at Anfield were flown at half-mast when he passed away in 2009. The Shankly Gates were opened so that his funeral cortege could take him on one last lap of his second home.

To Liverpool supporters who worship at Anfield every other week, the stadium is sacred and many a fan's last wish has been to have their ashes scattered on the hallowed turf. "A family came with a man's ashes when the ground was frost-bound," Shankly once recalled. "So the groundsman had the difficult job of digging a hole in the pitch inside the Kop net. He dug it a foot down at the right-hand side of the post facing the Kop and the casket containing the man's ashes was placed in it. So people not only support Liverpool when they're alive. They support them when they are dead."

So many ashes have been scattered by the Kop that when the club announced plans to move to a new stadium on Stanley Park during the early years of the 21st century, it was agreed that the

Above: Hand-painted wooden rattles, such as this, were a regular feature on the Kop during the immediate post-Second World War years.

Above right: A Liverpool Football Club supporter's rosette which was displayed with pride at matches during the 1980s.

proposed Anfield Plaza regeneration project would leave the pitch intact as sacrosanct ground.

Such devotion has come to demonstrate what being a Liverpool supporter is all about and that loyalty has been passed down through every generation of fans since. The Anfield crowd is also widely considered to be one of the most sporting, something that has only added to their legend.

After Arsenal snatched the league title from Liverpool's grasp in the most dramatic fashion in 1989, heartbroken home supporters stayed behind to applaud the new champions. "I looked out and saw the whole crowd clapping," recalled former Liverpool chief executive Peter Robinson. "I think the Arsenal players and fans were stunned by that."

It wasn't the first time the inhabitants of Anfield had hailed their team's conquerors. Two decades earlier, Leeds United, the Reds' fiercest rivals of the time, were afforded the same honour when a goalless draw in front of the Kop saw them crowned champions. It prompted their manager Don Revie to send a telegram expressing his club's gratitude. "Thanks for your very warm-hearted gesture. We nominate you as sportsmen of the century. You, your team and wonder manager deserve one another," it read.

Above all else, Anfield is famed as one of the world's most atmospheric sporting venues. Even if there wasn't much in the way of singing during the club's early years a raucous atmosphere could always be guaranteed. An article published in the *Liverpool Echo* in 1914 suggests spectator songs were a feature of games from 1906, the same year that the Kop was opened. More often than not, names of individual players would be shouted out. Harry Wilson started standing on the Kop in 1927 and when interviewed years later he recalled: "When Harry Chambers, our centre-forward, scored we'd all chant: 'Cham-bers, Cham-bers'.

He was one of our favourites. And then there was Elisha Scott, the greatest goalkeeper of them all. We called him Lisha. He was idolized by the Kop. They used to shout: 'Lisha, Lisha'."

In later years the songs booming out from the Kop often owed their origins to the pre-match pints consumed in one of the many public houses dotted around Anfield. "In our case it was always the Albert," says long-time Red Phil Aspinall. "If the songs were long we'd have to organise them. We'd usually do that before a game, while having a few drinks. If the words were easy and the tune was catchy, you might be able to start it that afternoon. Sometimes it would take a few games before it really got going."

In his sociological study of the game *The Soccer Tribe*, author Desmond Morris wrote: "During the 1960s when the chanting rituals first grew to epic proportions, the world of pop music was exploding in the cellars and clubs of Liverpool. The epoch of the Beatles had arrived and Merseyside awoke to find itself a centre of popular culture. The young fans of the Liverpool soccer terraces proudly took their new songs with them to the matches and gave mass renditions before the games, as a way of saying: 'We are the focus of today's music'. ... The scene was set for the merging of the different influences: the Victorian hymn singing, the Italian chanting, the South American clapping and shouting, and finally Beatlemania. They all came together on the sloping terraces of Liverpool's Spion Kop, and there a new tribal ritual was born, one which was to spread like wildfire from club to club across the land."

Journalists marvelled at the spontaneous wit and songwriting skills of the Anfield faithful. While stood in front of a swaying Kop in April 1964, a BBC reporter told viewers: "It used to be thought that Welsh international rugby crowds were the most musical and passionate in the world but I've never

> *"Anfield isn't a football ground, it's a sort of shrine. These people are not simply fans, they're more like members of one extended family."*
>
> **Bill Shankly**

seen anything like this Liverpool crowd. On the field here, the gay and inventive ferocity they show is quite stunning. The Duke of Wellington, before the battle of Waterloo, said of his own troops: 'I don't know what they do to the enemy but by God they frighten me,' and I'm sure some of the players here at this match must be feeling the same way."

Given their closer proximity to the fans than other players, goalkeepers have borne the brunt of the Kop's humour more than most.

Former Everton custodian Gordon West had the nickname "Honey West" bestowed on him, in reference to the famous actress of that name. Prior to one derby in the late 1960s, a supporter broke out of the Kop to present West with a personalized handbag bearing his new moniker. He took it in the good spirit it was meant and the handbag presentation became an annual ritual.

Leeds goalkeeper Gary Sprake also suffered at their hands. After he inadvertently threw the ball into his own net right as it squirmed from his grasp on an icy afternoon in December 1967, the home fans ensured he would never live it down. During the half-time break Des O'Connor's hit record of the time "Careless Hands" was aptly played over the loudspeakers and Kopites latched on to it straight away, serenading the crestfallen keeper for the remainder of the game.

Not all visiting number ones were on the sharp end of the Kop's rapier wit, however. England World Cup winner Gordon Banks was always guaranteed a warm reception, despite often proving a thorn in Liverpool's side during his time with Leicester and Stoke. He played his last ever game at Anfield in October 1972 before a car accident forced him to retire. On the opening day of the following season he was invited back as a guest of the club.

"They made a special presentation to me on the pitch and then Shankly and I did a lap of honour," he recalled. "Shanks gave me a Liverpool scarf, and I wrapped it around my neck. The Kop gave

me a wonderful reception. I don't mind admitting that I was a bit tearful. They were always very sporting. They obviously wanted their own team to win, but it never stopped them appreciating things the opposition might do. If they saw something special, they would applaud it."

Even players whom Liverpudlians loved to loathe were quickly forgiven the moment they pulled on the red shirt. In November 1959 staunch Reds threatened to boycott the club after Everton hero Dave Hickson made a controversial switch across Stanley Park. Despite the initial protests, a bumper crowd turned out for his debut against Aston Villa the following day with one supporter running across the pitch to greet him with a peck on the cheek. Hickson repaid the backing with both goals in a 2-1 Liverpool victory.

More recently, supporters displayed their humour by adapting the well-worn chant: "Attack, attack, attack" when a mystery moggy somehow found its way onto the pitch. The Kop responded to the incident – which came during a goalless draw with Spurs in February 2012 – with an immediate rendition of "a cat, a cat, a cat". Within 24 hours, the four-legged feline even had its own Twitter account @AnfieldCat!

Fans are fiercely proud of that spirit engendered over the years. In 2007 a group of like-minded Liverpudlians launched a campaign called "Reclaim the Kop" when sharing concerns that fan culture at Anfield was dipping below its usual high standards. It aimed to ensure future generations were brought up with the same ideals. According to its charter: "The Kop is a spirit, an attitude, the heart and soul of Liverpool F.C. No-one owns it, but together we are a legion, a force like no other." Also high on the RTK agenda was innovation. For instance, Liverpudlians have always been at the cutting edge of footballing fashions. From the suit-wearing, mop-topped crooners of the 1960s to the instigators of the designer sportswear revolution of the late 1970s and beyond, Anfield has always set the trends.

Clever banners for big European away games have long been par for the course for Liverpool supporters but in the 1990s, they also led the way with a series of organized "Flag Days" at Anfield. The first took place on the final Saturday of the 1992/93 season. It had been one of the worst campaigns in the Reds' recent history yet fans ensured it bowed out in a blaze of colour. "We were sitting in the Flat Iron on Walton Breck Road sometime in early 1993," recalls Kopite John Mackin, one of the chief organizers. "The campaign to save the old Kop look doomed so we turned our attention to seeing it off in style. As a prelude to the final farewell we organized a series of Flag Days so that by the time the last one came around against Norwich in 1994 everyone knew what to do. The response was amazing." Many more followed and nowadays one end of Anfield is always awash with flags and banners before every fixture. Since the turn of the millennium one flag, the brainchild of Kopite Frank Franceffa, is a regular visual accompaniment to the pre-match singing of "You'll Never Walk Alone". It measures 100ft x 65ft, weighs six stones and features 16-foot managers and 10-foot European trophies! The impressive spectacle is one to behold and the envy of others.

Match day mosaics became another Anfield first in the mid-1990s. Based on cards being held up by each fan, they have made for some spectacular sights. From a yellow "LFC" in 1995 to the words "Shanks", "GH", "The Kop 100", "The Truth" and "Sami" through to the 2014/15 season's display of the five European Cups, the mosaics have marked various events and anniversaries.

In 2014, excitement levels around Anfield grew as the team launched a serious assault to win its first ever Premier League title. Under the fresh managerial approach of Brendan Rodgers and with the enigmatic Luis Suarez leading the attack, the Reds had stormed to the top of the table and as the season entered its final straight there were unprecedented scenes outside the ground as fans lined the streets to welcome the team bus ahead of some crucial home games. The parades were organized by the Spion Kop 1906 group, with a spokesman stressing: "We don't do this for praise, we do it to generate an atmosphere in the ground and to make the Kop unique to anything else in this country."

With such a reputation, Anfield has become a sporting Mecca and a pilgrimage has become a key item on many people's bucket lists, including the rich and famous. After all, the pride and passion displayed during the last 130-odd years is conclusive evidence that when it comes to supporting their team, Kopites ensure that Liverpool Football Club never walks alone.

"*We don't do this for praise, we do it to generate an atmosphere in the ground and to make the Kop unique to anything else in this country.*"

'Spion Kop 1906' spokesman

Below: The back-to-back title-winning Liverpool team of the early 1920s pose for the cameras against the backdrop of supporters in the Main Stand Paddock.

Opposite: Liverpool supporters on a typically colourful Kop rack up the atmosphere a notch or two during the mid-1970s.

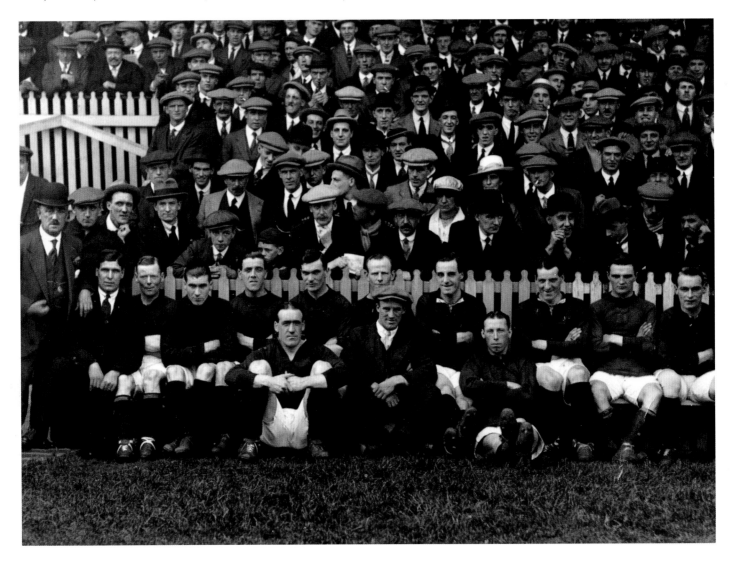

Left: The Spion Kop is a mass of scarves and flags as Ray Clemence and Phil Neal prepare for a league game against Arsenal in April 1979.

Opposite: Liverpool and Everton fans share a drink in the October sunshine before the Anfield derby of 1972–73. The Reds went home happier as Peter Cormack's goal secured a 1-0 win.

Below: The Liverpool team acknowledge the crowd before the European Super Cup final second leg against Kevin Keegan's Hamburg at Anfield in December 1977. The Reds won 6-0 to complete a 7-1 aggregate triumph.

Left: Boxing Day 1946 and after the gates are locked ahead of a crucial game with Stoke, supporters scale the walls of the Kop in an attempt to cheer on George Kay's champions-elect.

Below: Defender Phil Thompson is hugged by a jubilant fan who invaded the pitch to celebrate Liverpool's 2-1 aggregate win over Barcelona in the UEFA Cup semi-final at Anfield in 1976.

Far Below: Reds fans show their respect as Bob Paisley bows out as Liverpool manager in 1983 by celebrating the league title – his sixth in nine years as Reds boss.

Above left: Fans queue to gain entry to the standing Kop for the final time against Norwich City in April 1994. The Canaries won 1-0 but the supporters made it a memorable afternoon nonetheless.

Left: The Liverpool team bask in the glory of their club's 17th league title after a 1-0 win over Tottenham at Anfield in 1988.

Right: Captain Alan Hansen signs autographs as he walks down the players' tunnel during the glorious title-winning campaign of 1987/88.

"The Kop is a spirit, an attitude, the heart and soul of Liverpool F.C. No-one owns it, but together we are a legion, a force like no other."

'Reclaim The Kop' group spokesman

Above: Fans on the Kop unfurl flags before the final Premier League match of the 2014/15 season against Newcastle. Brendan Rodgers's men just fell short in their title challenge.

Above right: Jamie Carragher waves farewell to supporters after his 737th match for Liverpool against QPR in May 2013. He hit the woodwork in a 1-0 victory.

Right: Another incredible atmosphere for the Champions League semi-final second leg against Chelsea in 2007. Liverpool won 4-1 on penalties to reach their seventh European Cup final.

EVERY OTHER SATURDAY: ANFIELD 1928–1963

CHAPTER FOUR

EVERY OTHER SATURDAY: ANFIELD 1928–1963

The uncovered Spion Kop at Anfield was one of the most elevated and exposed sites in Liverpool. From the back it offered amazing panoramic views across the city, but it provided no shelter whatsoever from the extreme elements blown in from the Irish Sea.

This could be a pretty bleak and inhospitable place at times, especially when the team wasn't winning. Conditions were far from ideal, but this didn't deter the supporters from continually turning up in their droves every other week. Come wind, rain, hail or snow, the players never lacked support.

The late Billy O'Donnell attended his first game at Anfield in 1922. He was a long-time regular on the Kop and when interviewed in the early 1990s he recalled: "It was always cold and very windy. We all wore caps in those days in case it rained. And if you were standing down at the bottom of the Kop you needed to wear Wellingtons. Not

just because of the rain pouring down the Kop. But because of the toilet problem. You see, when you're stuck in the middle of the Kop and you've had a few pints before the match you have to get rid of it somehow. Well you can't go to the toilet, 'cos if you do you'll never get back and you certainly wouldn't find your mates again. So everybody used to do it there. They would bring a *Liverpool Echo* with them, roll it up and wee into it so that it didn't splash everybody!"

In 1928 the club's directors decided it was time to reward the loyalty of these hardy Kopites like Billy, who had happily stood on the uncomfortable slope created from a mound of cinder and ashes. The vast open terrace was redesigned, the steps were repaved in concrete and a roof put over it. "Those who pay their shilling to go on the Spion Kop have really been the backbone of the club," said new Chairman Tom Crompton. "Wet or fine

Previous pages: It's the summer of 1937 and the Liverpool team take time out before training to pose for a picture in front of the Main Stand.

Left: Liverpudlians brave the wind and the rain as they wait to enter the Spion Kop and Kemlyn Road turnstiles before a match at Anfield in 1957.

Righ: Cardiff-based pools company Sherman's produced a series called "Searchlight on Famous Teams", which included Liverpool's class of 1937/38. Matt Busby, future managerial mastermind of Manchester United, is third from left on the back row.

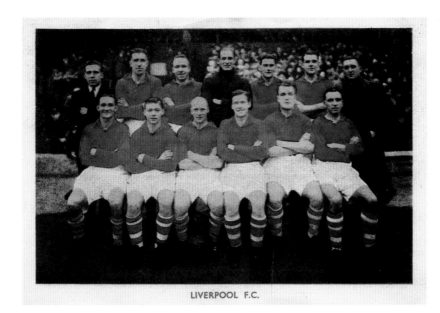

LIVERPOOL F.C.

▶ Two-thirds of its possible 28,000 spectators can see the game without a single intervening stanchion.

▶ The roof glazing is wirewoven, so that the spectators below are protected from broken glass, caused either by the wind or the ubiquitous small boy.

▶ If the steps of the Spion Kop were to be strung out in a line, that line would be longer than the length of the Liverpool Docks.

they have loyally filled their places and it has given great satisfaction to the directors to now make them as comfortable as possible with every protection against the inclement weather."

Surprisingly, it was a local architect and not Archibald Leitch who was approached by the club to spearhead the project. Crosby-based Joseph Cabre-Watson was a surprise choice given that his previous work had been predominantly in private housing, but his £38,000 design was unveiled to much acclaim and would soon become widely credited as being a key factor in many famous Liverpool victories.

Work to implement it took place during the summer of 1928. Once completed, it became the first roofed Kop in the country, enabling supporters to watch the game in more comfort while also amplifying the already raucous atmosphere generated by those who stood below. The new structure was a sight to behold and a special souvenir brochure was produced to commemorate its official opening. This highlighted a long list of the new Kop's standout features:

▶ It is 425 feet [130 metres] long by 131 feet [40 metres] wide, and is 80 feet [24 metres] high. A new stand in entirety, only the cinder hill beneath the centre portion and three post-war staircases now remain of the old Kop of two years ago.

It was inaugurated by Football League President John McKenna, a man steeped in Anfield tradition. As a former Liverpool secretary and director, he had played a significant role in the development of the ground during the club's formative years. Now proud to see what great strides had been made off the field, he nonetheless warned that it should never be to the detriment of what happens on it: "Stay your hands in the matter of further improvements of the ground and devote your finances, energy and intelligence to creating a team worthy of its splendid ground accommodation."

The first opponents to play in front of the imposing new covered terrace were Bury. Their ranks included future Liverpool captain Tom "Tiny" Bradshaw, but he was unable to prevent the Reds running out 3-0 winners, with Ballymena-born Billy Millar scoring the first goal after just one minute of his Reds' debut.

Anfield could now offer more covered accommodation than any other ground in the Football League. In addition to the new roof, 600 new seats were added to an extended Main Stand that now joined up with the Kop, while an extra 200 seats were installed in the Kemlyn Road. The overall capacity had been increased by about

Above left: In March 1932 Liverpool's Jimmy McDougall lined up against his brother Jack when Sunderland visited Anfield for a match in which the visitors ran out 2-1 winners.

Above right: During the 1930s and '40s Anfield was a popular venue for boxing, hosting a total of 148 bouts, including two world title fights. Pictured here are Freddie Miller and Nel Tarleton contest the World Featherweight title in June 1934.

7,000, meaning there was now ample room to house over 60,000 fans.

At the same time that the new Kop roof was being unveiled, the club announced plans for further improvements and they published a sketch for a proposed double-decker stand at the Anfield Road end. Maybe the directors heeded the wise words of McKenna, though, because like the "hat-trick stand" idea of a few years earlier, it never did come to fruition.

Nevertheless, with an increased capacity, the ground's record attendance was broken twice in the space of the next six years, both for FA Cup ties. In February 1932, 57,804 saw Chelsea end Liverpool's Wembley aspirations at the quarter-final stage, and on 27 January 1934, 61,036 watched a fourth-round tie against Tranmere Rovers.

That was the season Anfield bade an emotional farewell to one of its favourite sons. After a distinguished 22 years keeping goal for the Reds, Elisha Scott announced that he would be returning to his native Belfast. Very few players have been so loved by the fans and on the afternoon of Liverpool's final home game, Scott took the unprecedented step of addressing the crowd from the directors' box to thank them for their support.

Scott's departure added to the depression that was beginning to shroud Anfield. In a climate of economic downturn, Liverpool's fortunes followed a similar path. On the field the team lurched perilously towards the lower reaches of Division One and, apart from the aforementioned big cup ties or derby games, the number of supporters coming through the turnstiles was starting to tail off significantly.

Since the previous decade Anfield had also been the finishing point for the Liverpool Marathon, with the runners completing a lap of the ground during the club's annual pre-season practice match.

Now, in a bid to boost the club's finances, the gates were opened to a number of other sporting events, particularly boxing. Between 1931 and 1949, a total of 27 shows, featuring 148 bouts, were staged in front of the Kop. One of the most famous contests took place on 20 September 1934, when 31,213 fans saw local favourite Nel Tarleton narrowly miss out on the World Featherweight title, losing on points to America's Freddie Miller. Four years later another world title fight saw Peter Kane claim the flyweight belt against Jackie Jurich.

In June 1937 Anfield had also staged the deciding round of a star-studded professional tennis tournament. Boards were put down on the pitch and the legendary Fred Perry, a three-time Wimbledon and US Open champion, went up against Ellsworth Vines, an American believed to be the world's best. After losing the first set, Stockport-born Perry came back to win the match 3-1. He and Vines then paired up to play a doubles game against Bill Tilden and Lester Stoefen.

Although these other sporting ventures proved successful, they would never usurp football in the popularity stakes at Anfield, and in the wake of the Second World War, supporters came flocking back in record numbers. For the first time in Anfield history the average gate topped 40,000 as Liverpool defied the odds to clinch a fifth Football League Championship in 1946/47. The following

Above: Liverpool players (left to right) Bobby Savage, Fred Howe, Vic Wright, Ben Dabbs and Fred Rogers set off on a training walk from the Main Stand car park in 1936.

year, even a schoolboy game was watched by an incredible 48,000.

Heading into the 1950s, the team was back on a downward spiral, but in February 1952 Anfield was bursting at the seams as a new record crowd of 61,905 squeezed into the ground for a FA Cup fourth-round tie against Wolves (see page 69).

Encouraged by this rise in attendances, the Liverpool directors instructed a local firm of architects to draw up plans for an ambitious redevelopment project that involved the construction of a new triple-decker stand to replace Anfield Road enclosure. As you can see from the drawing on page 74, the vision shown was impressive.

The idea harked back to the one first mooted in the 1920s, and had this stand been built, Anfield's capacity would have soared to near 70,000, making it one of the biggest and, arguably, best grounds in the country. In the club minute books, no explanation is given for why the plans did not proceed, but the likelihood is that following the team's relegation in 1954 made the board got cold feet and the directors decided to err on the side of caution.

They did invest £12,000 to install floodlights, though, and these were switched on for the first time against Everton in October 1957. A 3-2 victory over their top-flight neighbours was a boost to morale but not enough to overturn a 2-0 first-leg deficit in the aptly named Floodlit Challenge Cup, awarded to celebrate the 75th anniversary of the Liverpool County FA. The advent of floodlights put an end to the tradition of midweek games kicking off in the afternoon or early evening. It also instigated a whole new change in the match-going culture of supporters; as would become evident in later decades, playing under lights added an exciting new

dimension to the game, especially at Anfield.

Thankfully, the directors also saw the light in footballing terms. Five years of directionless stagnation in Division Two was starting to hit them in the pocket. Dwindling gates set the alarm bells ringing, and in 1959 Bill Shankly was brought in as manager. His brief was simple: to bring the glory days back to Anfield. The ambitious Scot wanted to build a dynasty, but it was clear that there was plenty of work to be done on and off the pitch before Liverpool could even think about competing at the top level again.

On first inspection of the ground the new boss was not impressed, describing Anfield as "the biggest toilet in Liverpool". The toilets, though, didn't even flush and there was no running water in the changing rooms. Although Anfield was on standby to stage the 1958 FA Cup final replay between Manchester United and Bolton Wanderers if they had drawn at Wembley, the ground had fallen into a sorry state of disrepair. On the crumbling concrete steps grass had been allowed to grow, while the woodwork hadn't experienced a lick of paint for years.

Shankly was to play a significant role in stopping the rot. Promotion was achieved in 1962. A 2-0 victory at home to Southampton clinched that long-awaited return to the top flight and amid the wild celebrations that followed, Ron Yeats and Ian St John, two of his key new signings, were joyously dragged into a resurgent Kop. Terrace culture was changing and Kopites were at the forefront, leading the way with their rhythmic clapping and innovative chanting. They suddenly had new heroes to cheer, giving rise to the birth of the legendary Kop choir and Anfield's reputation as one of the most atmospheric grounds in Europe.

GREAT GAME
Liverpool v Wolverhampton Wanderers, FA Cup fourth round
2 February 1952

Anfield has long been synonymous with big crowds, but none was bigger than the 61,905 that packed into the ground for this memorable fourth round FA Cup tie with Wolverhampton Wanderers.

Liverpool had yet to win the trophy and everyone connected to the club was desperate to see them finally prevail. Just two years earlier, the Reds had lost to Arsenal in the final on their first ever appearance at Wembley, and the aim now was to get back there and go one better.

After beating Workington in round three, this was a much tougher draw. Although both sides sat mid-table in the League, separated only by goal average, Wolves were regarded as one of the top teams of the day. They had won the cup three times in the past and never lost a tie to Liverpool.

It was undoubtedly one of the standout games of the round and the demand for stand tickets was so great that an editorial in the matchday programme revealed they could have been sold eight times over.

Those lucky enough to see the action witnessed a Liverpool victory that can be attributed to a tactical masterstroke by manager Don Welsh. Having got wind of how Wolves planned to nullify the threat of outside left Billy Liddell, Welsh instructed Liddell to switch positions with centre-forward Cyril Done once the game kicked off.

It worked a treat. By the time the visitors realized what had happened, Liverpool were two goals to the good, thanks to strikes from Bob Paisley and Done inside the first nine minutes. Jimmy Mullen netted a consolation for Wolves after half-time, but it wasn't enough.

Liverpool progressed, only to see their cup aspirations ended in the next round. The attendance against Wolves, however, has yet to be surpassed. And unless Anfield is expanded beyond what is already planned, it's a record that's set to remain intact.

Right: The official programme for the game against Wolverhampton Wanderers in February 1952 that attracted a club record crowd of 61,905.

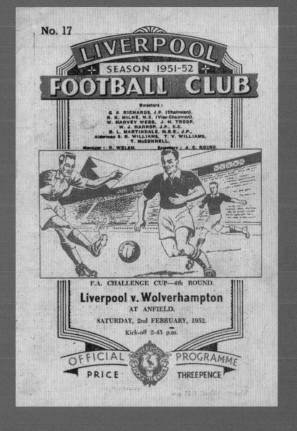

"*Those who pay their shilling to go on the Spion Kop have really been the backbone of the club. Wet or fine they have loyally filled their places and it has given great satisfaction to the directors to now make them as comfortable as possible with every protection against the inclement weather.*"

Tom Crompton, Liverpool Football Club Chairman

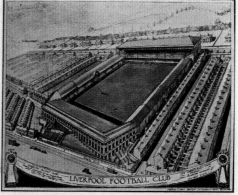

Liverpool Football Club.

(Sketch shows also the proposed Anfield Road New Stand).

OPENING OF SPION KOP NEW STAND

—— by ——

The President of the English Football League, etc.,

JOHN McKENNA, Esq.

At 3-0 p.m. on SATURDAY, AUGUST 25th, 1928, prior to

THE OPENING GAME—LIVERPOOL v. BURY.

Above: The newly roofed Spion Kop pictured ahead of its official opening on 25 August 1928, an occasion Liverpool marked by beating Bury 3-0. In the bottom left of this picture you can just see the corner of the first Boys' Pen.

Right: The brochure published to commemorate the opening of the new Spion Kop in 1928. It featured a sketch of how the club proposed to further develop the ground in future years.

Above: Harman Van Den Berg, Ben Dabbs (on the bench), Willie Fagan, Phil Taylor, Berry Nieuwenhuys on the bars, and Matt Busby in the gymnasium beneath Anfield's Main Stand during the 1938/39 season.

THE SEASON'S SPECIAL

SAVE MONEY
and Invest in a
WAR SAVINGS CERTIFICATE
by Buying a
MEMBER'S SEASON TICKET
for 1943/4.
Price £2 : 0 : 0 (INCLUDING TAX)

Admits holder to a seat in CENTRE STAND.
For all League Matches, Cup Ties, and 2nd Team Matches.

LIVERPOOL F.C. FIXTURES.

1943.		
Aug. 28—MANCHESTER CITY	...	HOME
Sept. 4—Manchester City	...	Away
,, 11—WREXHAM	...	HOME
,, 18—Wrexham	...	Away
,, 25—BURY	...	HOME
Oct. 2—Bury	...	Away
,, 9—Everton	...	Away
,, 16—EVERTON	...	HOME
,, 23—MANCHESTER UNITED	...	HOME
,, 30—Manchester United	...	Away
Nov. 6—Chester	...	Away
,, 13—CHESTER	...	HOME
,, 20—SOUTHPORT	...	HOME
,, 27—Southport	...	Away
Dec. 4—BURNLEY	...	HOME
,, 11—Burnley	...	Away
,, 18—Tranmere Rovers	...	Away
,, 25—TRANMERE ROVERS	...	HOME

Left: A single-sheet issue of the match day programme produced for a war-time game between Liverpool and Everton that was played to raise money for the Lord Mayor of Liverpool's War Fund.

Below: A postcard to Les Yell from George Patterson calling him to attend a reserve team fixture against Lytham at Anfield on 11 February 1938.

Far below: Captain Jack Balmer leads the Reds out, closely followed by future manager Phil Taylor and Ray Lambert, sometime during the late 1940s when Anfield experienced a post-war attendance boom.

Liverpool Association Football Club.
ANFIELD ROAD, ANFIELD.

NATIONAL TEL.
134 ANFIELD.   TELS. "GOALKEEPER LIVERPOOL."

Dear Sir,

You are selected to play v.

at   on

Train leaves

Kick-off

Meet at

Yours truly,

George Patterson
Secretary and Manager

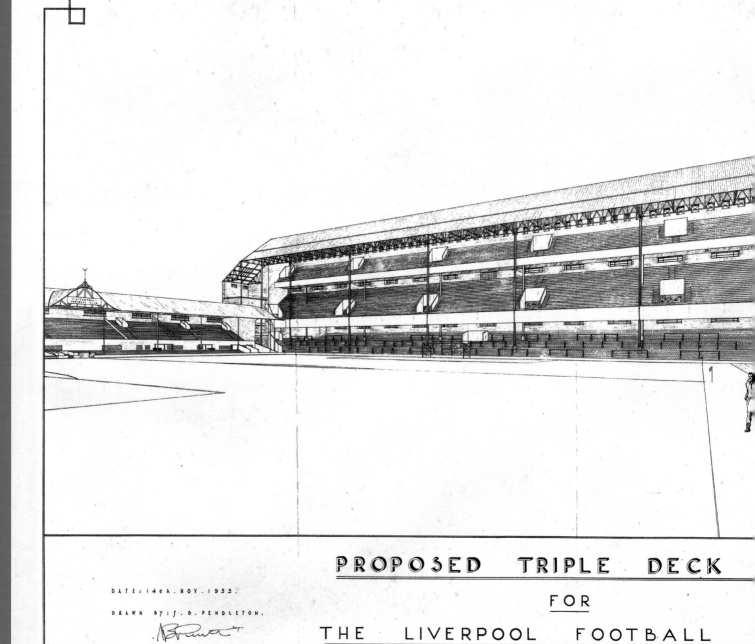

PROPOSED TRIPLE DECK

FOR

THE LIVERPOOL FOOTBALL

DATE: 14th. NOV. 1955.

DRAWN BY: J. B. PENDLETON.

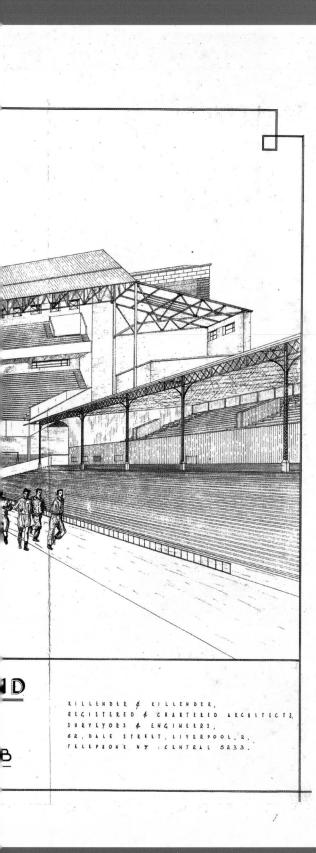

PROPOSED TRIPLE DECK STAND

FOR

THE LIVERPOOL FOOTBALL CLUB

Left: In the 1950s Liverpool commissioned a local firm of architects to draw up plans for an ambitious triple-decker stand at the Anfield Road end. The idea was first mooted three decades earlier but for reasons unknown was never built.

Above: The exterior view of the proposed "hat-trick" stand, complete with a row of shops underneath. These plans were drawn by Jack Pendleton on behalf of a Dale Street based company called Killender & Killender.

KILLENDER & KILLENDER,
REGISTERED & CHARTERED ARCHITECTS,
SURVEYORS & ENGINEERS,
62, DALE STREET, LIVERPOOL, 2,
TELEPHONE N° : CENTRAL 5233.

> *"There's no noise like the Anfield noise, and I love it."*
>
> Ian St John

Above: A cloth badge bearing the logo used during the 1960s. The patch dates from the middle of that decade, around the time the Reds won their first FA Cup.

Right: Liverpool's players celebrate their 1963/64 title triumph in front of the Anfield Road end following a 5-0 victory over Arsenal.

STAND 4½

Above: The swashbuckling "Sir" Roger Hunt ensured fans at Anfield had plenty to shout about between 1959 and 1969, scoring what was then a club record 285 goals.

Left: Supporters queue outside the Kop, on the corner of Kemlyn Road in 1956. Despite being in the Second Division at this time, Liverpool could still regularly attract big crowds.

Below: The official programme for Liverpool's Floodlit Challenge Cup game against Everton in 1959, a game that took place almost two years to the day since the Reds first played under lights at Anfield.

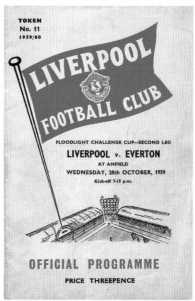

TOKEN
No. 11
1959/60

LIVERPOOL
FOOTBALL CLUB

FLOODLIGHT CHALLENGE CUP—SECOND LEG
LIVERPOOL v. EVERTON
AT ANFIELD
WEDNESDAY, 28th OCTOBER, 1959
Kick-off 7-15 p.m.

OFFICIAL PROGRAMME

PRICE THREEPENCE

Above: A late 1960s view looking down the access steps up to the Spion Kop stand at the corner of the Kemlyn Road and Walton Breck Road.

Left: Fans in the Main Stand have a great vantage point as flying winger Peter Thompson crosses during a 1-1 draw against Burnley on Boxing Day 1968.

ANFIELD LEGEND
BILL **SHANKLY**

The presence of Bill Shankly will forever loom large at Anfield. The man who led the club into its most successful era is honoured in the form of commemorative gates and a bronze statue. Given the influence he exerted on and off the pitch during his 15 years at Liverpool, they are richly deserved.

He was recruited from Huddersfield Town in December 1959, and it was his vision that dragged the club kicking and screaming from the relative obscurity of Division Two to the forefront of the game, both in this country and beyond.

At the same time he connected with the fans like no other and acted as their representative in the boardroom. Though he described Anfield as "the biggest toilet in Liverpool" shortly after his arrival at the club, it quickly became his spiritual home, and he said later, "The very word 'Anfield' means more to me than I can describe."

Shanks strived to make it a venue befitting his team of champions – and he succeeded. As well as a multitude of trophies, his time in charge also saw the construction of three new stands, the introduction of the famous "This Is Anfield" sign and the birth of the legendary Kop choir, of which he was the orchestrator-in-chief.

By the time he departed in 1974, the club had changed beyond all recognition. Seven years later Anfield mourned his passing during a European Cup tie at home to Oulun Pallosuera. The flag on the Great Eastern flagpole flew at half-mast, the players wore black armbands and the crowd fell eerily silent. Despite a 7-0 win, the football seemed irrelevant and for almost the entire second half fans on the Kop paid their own special tribute to the great man by incessantly chanting his name.

As the inscription on his statue says, "He made the people happy", and, even now, his spirit continues to touch every aspect of life at Anfield.

Left: Bill Shankly acknowledges the Anfield crowd after being presented with his Manager of the Year award for 1973, the year in which he guided the Reds to UEFA Cup success and the First Division title.

Right: Shanks points the way to success in an iconic image taken in front of the Main Stand in 1961.

"The very word 'Anfield' means more to me than I can describe."
Bill Shankly

BEHIND THE SCENES: ANFIELD'S UNSUNG HEROES

CHAPTER FIVE

BEHIND THE SCENES: ANFIELD'S UNSUNG HEROES

Throughout the course of Liverpool Football Club's rich history, names like Shankly, Paisley, Gerrard, Dalglish, Liddell, Callaghan and many more trip off the tongue when people think of the men who have helped make the Reds great.

Their contributions to Anfield are woven into the rich tapestry of LFC and rightly so. But they would be among the first to acknowledge that their efforts don't begin to tell the whole story.

All were steeped in the mantra that no-one was bigger than the club and Liverpool has always flourished because, with its individuals working together, it is greater than the sum of its parts.

Underpinning the success of those great players and managers in L4 were unsung heroes who worked tirelessly behind the scenes. In a way they were the Anfield backbenchers and civil servants, poring over the small details to provide a platform for the club to conquer at home and abroad. To find the first of these men you have to go back to the very start.

When John Houlding decided to create a new team to play at Anfield following Everton's decision to leave, he asked close friend William Barclay to back the venture. Local businessman John McKenna was also invited to join Liverpool Football Club's first committee and their early efforts were essential in paving the way for the club to grow.

As well as a sharp eye for administrative detail, their responsibilities included the playing side of the club. Barclay was "secretary/manager" as Liverpool took its first steps while McKenna appears to have been more a "coach/manager".

Barclay's contribution should never be overlooked. It was he who suggested the very name Liverpool Association Football Club to Houlding before helping create its first great side: the "Team of all the Macs".

Born in the Kilmainham Auxiliary of the South Dublin Workhouse on 14 June 1857, Barclay had been involved in the early days of Everton Football Club and served as vice-president prior to being named vice-chairman in June 1890. However, he tendered his resignation from the Toffees in September 1891 after they rejected Houlding's resolution to form the club into a limited liability company.

Barclay stayed loyal to Houlding and his wish to create a new footballing power on Merseyside. His sterling service at Anfield also saw him appointed as executive of the Lancashire FA in 1893. However, few were aware that his footballing feats were taking place against a backdrop of personal problems with wife, Emily, battling illness. In August 1896, Liverpool took the bold decision to appoint the successful Sunderland manager Tom Watson as secretary-manager in place of Barclay, who sadly lost touch with the footballing community in his later years.

Barclay passed away in 1917. Sadly, he was buried in a pauper's grave and there was no mention of his death in Liverpool Football Club's minute books. It was a tragic end for someone whose role had been so crucial to the foundation of the club. Concerned that history would not remember him as it should, football historians and keen Liverpool supporters George Rowlands and Jonny Stokkeland commissioned a new headstone which was placed on his grave at Anfield Cemetery in November 2012.

McKenna, meanwhile, was a footballing visionary who was not about to wait for LFC to take their place at the top table of the English game. At the end of their very first season in the Lancashire League, he wrote to the FA – seemingly without anyone's knowledge – requesting election to the Football League. Due to the old Test Match system, and no automatic promotion, Liverpool played off against the Football League's bottom-placed club Newton Heath (now known as Manchester United). They eased to a 2-0 victory and thus achieved First Division status.

McKenna later had two spells as Liverpool Chairman: 1909–1914 and 1917–1919. He stayed on as a director until July 1921. One of the great early administrators of the English game, McKenna was elected to the Football League's management committee in 1902, becoming vice-president in 1908 and President two years later. He held the latter position until his death in Walton Hospital in 1936.

Everton Chairman, Will Cuff, said: "From the Football League and Football Association's point of view I think the greatest man in football has gone.

Fearless, outspoken, and absolutely honest, he was well named "Honest John". The football world in general is under a very deep sorrow."

A commemorative brass wall plaque in McKenna's honour has been housed at Anfield for many years and will be redisplayed when the rebuilt Main Stand opens in 2016.

The foundations laid by Barclay and McKenna were built on by others and the club is rightly proud that some of the most able officials in English football have been employed at Anfield.

Another was George Patterson who, in essence, ran the club following the death of Tom Watson in 1915. Patterson had been appointed assistant secretary in 1908 and took over the leadership of the Liverpool team after Watson's passing but was not officially appointed as manager until September 1918. *Liverpool Echo* journalist Ernest "Bee" Edwards announced: "I am glad that Mr George Patterson has been appointed secretary of Liverpool FC. He is a practical man, unobtrusive, and shows wisdom with pen and in football matters."

Patterson led the Reds through wartime's chaotic local competitions. Despite players being stationed all over the country and beyond, he always managed to field competitive teams and blooded youngsters such as Harry Chambers and Tommy Lucas who would each play more than 300 games for Liverpool.

When league football resumed in 1919/20, a distinction was made between secretary and manager. David Ashworth and Matt McQueen succeeded Patterson in looking after team affairs but he reluctantly resumed control again in March

1928. It perhaps says more about the lack of importance then placed on the role of manager that when the position was discussed at the club's annual meeting in 1936, the board wanted Patterson to focus on administrative matters "because the value of secretarial work was growing enormously." Patterson's contribution to the club is often underplayed but he was a key figure in the smooth running of its operations during the inter-war period.

The acumen demonstrated in administration extended to the Anfield boardroom. Forward-thinking Bill McConnell served as director and Chairman from 1928 to 1947 and is widely considered to have been the brains behind the Reds' title success in the first post-war league season of 1946/47. A caterer by trade with a string of dockside cafes, "Billy Mac" proposed that the team should escape food-rationed Britain and embark on a pre-season tour of North America. He was convinced of the nutritional benefits of such a trip and was vindicated when the team defied all odds to claim the championship.

Another who saw the bigger picture was Thomas Valentine Williams, a member of the Anfield boardroom for almost 30 years in the capacities of Director, Chairman and President. During the early 1950s he advocated the purchase of an unkempt school field in West Derby, which duly became known as Melwood, the club's training ground. He also played a big part in forming the Boot Room dynasty of Bob Paisley, Reuben Bennett and Joe Fagan, but the biggest legacy left by "TV" was his appointment of Bill Shankly as manager in 1959.

Keen to build on Shankly's naked ambition was director Eric Sawyer. A shrewd accountant, he was recommended to the Anfield board by John Moores, having aided him in the building of his Littlewoods empire. When Shankly sensed the club did not match his own vision for creating a team capable of competing for the biggest honours, Sawyer was an important ally. Shanks told the board that the club "could not afford not to sign Ron Yeats and Ian St John". In May 1961, with the adequate funds eventually made available, Liverpool smashed their transfer record to sign the Saint and the Reds were on their way to glory with "Rowdy" following a couple of months later, being installed as captain before the year was out.

John Smith, Chairman between 1973 and 1990, was another whose impact sometimes flies beneath the radar. He oversaw the club's greatest period of success and was a key advocate of the policy of promoting from within. He also led Liverpool into the commercial era by brokering a groundbreaking shirt sponsorship deal with Japanese electronics conglomerate Hitachi in 1979.

In the years since, David Moores and Rick Parry smoothed the way for further triumphs while Martin Broughton played a brief but significant role as Chairman in 2010, helping to rescue the Reds from the brink of bankruptcy by finding new owners in New England Sports Ventures [now Fenway Sports Group] following the ill-fated ownership of Tom Hicks and George Gillett.

As seen in the case of William Barclay, however, the stories of some of the club's unsung are tinged with sadness. The growth of the game in the post-war era took its toll in the ultimately tragic story of Jimmy McInnes. A left-half who played 51 games for the Reds after joining from Third Lanark in

> *"Gerry [Marsden] told me that they used to play the Top 10 records before kick-off at Anfield but when YNWA fell out of the chart, lots of people complained. So it carried on being played and just snowballed from there."*
>
> Anfield announcer George Sephton

1938, the Scot seemed set for a lengthy playing career at Anfield until war intervened. By the time competitive football resumed he had joined the club's office staff, working his way up to secretary. He went about his business in an understated and conscientious manner but Liverpool's successes under Shankly increased his heavy workload and brought intolerable stress. The day after the 1965 European Cup semi-final first leg against Inter Milan, McInnes was found hanging in a turnstile enclosure at the back of the Kop.

McInnes had been known for his quiet and kind demeanour and the Reds replaced him with a man chiselled from the same stone. While the club was revered for its triumphs on the pitch it also came to be admired for the manner it conducted itself off it. Driving that modus operandi was Peter Robinson, who handled matters with the utmost dignity, humility and minimum of fuss. Recruited from Brighton after the club's first FA Cup success in the summer of 1965, he proved to be a safe pair of hands to deal with the mountain of paperwork that came with the Reds' rise in status to one of Europe's most successful sides. Never one to seek the limelight he worked as secretary until 1992 then chief executive to 2000, pioneering the "Liverpool Way" in the modern era.

By the time "PBR" came on board, Liverpool were enjoying their first tastes of European football. As time went on, part of his ever-expanding role involved the meticulous planning of the club's travel arrangements. He was a close confidant of Shankly and Dalglish, with the latter revealing that in those pre-transfer-window days, Robinson endeavoured to make funds available for new recruits as soon as the old tax year ended. This enabled the Reds to steal a march on their rivals by securing signings during April and May.

Robinson was a rock for the club during the tough times that followed Heysel and Hillsborough and

Dalglish paid tribute to the team behind the team in his autobiography, explaining: "Liverpool's secret was that they employed the best; the best tea-ladies and the best administrator in Peter Robinson."

That philosophy also extended to groundstaff. While others were busy creating the conditions conducive to on-field glories, Arthur Riley did so literally! In the never-to-be-forgotten 1988 record "The Anfield Rap", midfielder Craig Johnston's lyrics included the classic line: "Pass and move, it's the Liverpool groove". A key factor in developing that motto had been the cultivation of a luxurious playing surface. "We have great grass at Anfield," Shankly once remarked. "Professional grass!" That wasn't always the case – in the 1890s the club took out an advert in the local press looking for sheep to graze on the pitch!

For almost three-quarters of the 20th century, the responsibilities for tending to the playing surface were held by the Riley family. Bert Riley was groundsman from 1908 but had little help in the way of assistants. In preparation for each new season he would recruit his children to lend a hand. One of them, Arthur, recalled: "We used stiff brushes to clean down the seats which then consisted of long benches with iron partitions." Not to be confused with the ex-Reds goalkeeper of the same name, Arthur was bitten by the bug. In 1928, he joined the club straight from school. When Bert passed away in 1950, Arthur succeeded him as the Anfield groundsman maintaining the club's policy of continuity.

"I learned a great deal from my father in the years I worked with him," Arthur recalled. "I'll never forget one Friday night when we both got out of bed after midnight to tend the pitch. We got news that it was starting to freeze so it was vital to flatten the surface before that happened. So there we were rolling the ground in the moonlight in the early hours of the morning."

A hugely popular figure within the club during his lengthy tenure, he was involved in the upkeep of the hallowed Anfield turf for 54 years. Such was his reputation for maintaining the pitch to the highest standards that Wembley groundstaff often sought his advice. Arthur witnessed many advances including the installation of floodlights in 1957 and undersoil heating just before his retirement in 1982. He took great pride in Anfield being considered one of the finest playing surfaces in the country and constantly strove to keep it in immaculate condition.

During his earlier days, the groundstaff received some help from the Reds' apprentices. Jimmy Melia was a case in point. Growing up in a small terraced house in Scotland Road as one of 11 children, he joined the Liverpool groundstaff in 1952, aged 15. Melia was one of a dozen youngsters placed under the command of Bob Paisley, the recently retired wing-half. "In the summertime when the first-team players were off, we'd help paint the ground," Melia recalled. "Later, we would go down to Melwood and dig six feet down so we could fit floodlights into the turf. It was hard labour but it made sure there were no big-heads."

In a city that had become as well known for its music as its football, the playing of records naturally became an essential part of the entertainment at Anfield. The Mersey Sound of the sixties had provided the soundtrack to the success of Shankly's early Liverpool teams and as the sixties became the seventies, there was a change of match day disc jockey – a switch that would have a significant impact on generations of Reds.

For almost 45 years, listening to George Sephton's dulcet tones has been part of the match-going experience at Anfield. George received his big break after writing to Peter Robinson in the early 1970s, claiming he could do a better job than the resident DJ! George assumed control of the decks for the first game of the 1971/72 season against Nottingham Forest and has missed only a handful of matches since. During that time, he has kept supporters informed and entertained, with his duties including reading out the teams, passing on important messages and notifying supporters of other scores from around the grounds. He has also been a keen promoter of local bands.

Of course, a key role is the playing of the Kop anthem "You'll Never Walk Alone" prior to kick-off. Speaking to the match day programme in 2013 on the 50th anniversary of Gerry Marsden's classic being released, George explained: "Gerry told me that they used to play the Top 10 records before kick-off at Anfield but when YNWA fell out of the chart, lots of people complained. So it carried on being played and just snowballed from there."

Of course, there are countless more people who have contributed in so many ways throughout the club's incredible journey to date, but these are just some of the unheralded figures who have helped make Anfield so special.

> *"Liverpool's secret is that they employed the best; the best tea-ladies and the best administrator in Peter Robinson."*
> **Kenny Dalglish**

Left: The calm before the storm underneath the Centenary Stand as an Anfield programme seller gets ready for the usual pre-match rush.

Below: The view from Anfield's TV gantry, taken in September 1990 during a game against Manchester United.

Opposite: Polishing the family silver. Former LFC cleaner May Devine pictured with the League Championship trophy in May 1980, shortly before placing it into the Anfield trophy cabinet.

Left: Player turned coach Ephraim Longworth hard at work in a later role on the club's groundstaff. A Liverpool captain, he made 371 appearances during his playing career.

Below: Groundsman Reg Summers oversees the complete relaying of the Anfield playing surface during the summer of 1998.

Opposite: A member of the groundstaff takes a breather between cuts of the grass on the corner of the Main Stand and Anfield Road.

"*I learned a great deal from my father ...
I'll never forget one Friday night when
we both got out of bed after midnight
to tend the pitch.*"

Arthur Riley, former Anfield groundsman

"We have great grass at Anfield ... Professional grass!"

Bill Shankly

Right: High-tech equipment is put in place ahead of work to ensure the club's playing surface remains one of the best in the game.

A FIELD OF DREAMS:
THE PLAYING EXPERIENCE

CHAPTER SIX

A FIELD OF DREAMS
THE PLAYING EXPERIENCE

Lining up in the narrow tunnel before kick-off, hearing the opening chords of "You'll Never Walk Alone" strike up, touching the famous This Is Anfield sign and walking out on to the green, green grass of home with the Liverbird upon your chest.

To Liverpool supporters, just imagining what that must be like sends shivers down the spine. Only a privileged number have lived this dream. None more so than Ian Callaghan the club's record appearance holder with an incredible 857 matches to his name, a statistic reached over 17 seasons of playing regularly at Anfield. He describes the Reds' headquarters as a temple of emotion. "When we talk about Anfield, it immediately summons up visions of the Kop in full, raucous voice and thrilling football moments.

For Cally the thrill of playing in front of a packed house was even more special as a he was a local lad who went on to represent the club he had grown up supporting. The same was true of Steven Gerrard, who left Liverpool in the summer of 2015 having been a fixture in the first team set-up for almost 17 years.

He recalled having his appetite whetted the first time he set foot in the stadium, having been taken along to a League Cup tie against Coventry City in November 1986, aged six.

"The first time I went to Anfield will always stand out in my mind. Steve Heighway invited me along and sorted out the tickets for us in the old Kemlyn Road stand [now the Centenary Stand]. The main thing I can remember is the excitement when I heard the turnstiles click. I can remember the floodlights dazzling my eyes because it was a night game, and the green colour of the pitch. It looked amazing and gave me such a buzz. Then there was the smell of Bovril – everyone seemed to be drinking it at half-time!

"It was a strange game; Jan Molby scored three penalties. But that was my first taste of what real football was about with big stadiums and big crowds. I realized there was an

expectation on the players. It gave me more hunger to study the game and follow Liverpool even more closely."

He certainly did that! No-one has captained Liverpool more often than Gerrard, who led them on an incredible 470 occasions. After his initial appointment back in October 2003, he spoke of his thrill at being asked to lead Liverpool out on a regular basis. "The manager has always said that I would captain Liverpool Football Club one day but it was a bit of a shock when Gerard [Houllier] told me I was to be captain from now on. I have to say I'm absolutely thrilled.

"I was captain of my school side and I used to go along to Anfield to watch the team and always

Above: Goalkeeper Ray Clemence acknowledges the crowd ahead of his testimonial game against Anderlecht in May 1980. "Clem" enjoyed a strong relationship with the Kop.

looked up to people like John Barnes who captained the team during the 1990s. I used to watch Barnes with the captain's armband and dream that one day it would be me captaining the team I love. I'm delighted to be captain of Liverpool Football Club and thrilled to be representing the fans on the pitch."

While the love of Liverpool was ingrained in a number of local lads, there was also a special relationship forged with a group of players who joined after arriving from far foreign lands. Who can forget Sami Hyypia shedding a few tears in 2009 as the Kop sang his name while he was held aloft by team-mates following his final game for the Reds? Xabi Alonso, another Champions League winner with Liverpool in 2005, had a similar story. The Basque boy from Tolosa became a firm favourite during a five-season spell which established a bond that the midfielder says will last a lifetime.

Speaking in 2011, he revealed: "I am still a Liverpool fan and will be for ever. The things that I have lived and the experiences I had during those five years are deep in my heart and the passion and respect I had for the club and its supporters are still the same. Hopefully I can transmit to my son what Liverpool Football Club means and how special it is, as he was born in the city."

More recently, Luis Suarez wrote his name on to the list of the best players to have worn the famous red jersey. The Uruguayan was handed the number-seven shirt on his arrival from Ajax in 2011, a number steeped in history at Anfield and worn by legends such as Kevin Keegan and Kenny Dalglish. "When I got the number seven I was happy because I knew it was a historic number that various top players had worn throughout the club's history," he said. "But the number I've got on the back of my shirt is the last thing on my mind when I go out to play.

"Something I learnt from a very young age early on in my football career was that you never give up. You never give up on a ball as a lost cause, you fight for everything … you never drop your head for one minute and you keep trying until the last whistle. You do that for the team and for the supporters. To stand on the pitch and look at the Kop when it's full is spectacular. Not just the Kop, but all of Anfield."

The value of that relationship between players and the Anfield supporters is something you cannot place a value on. John Toshack, the 1970s star who forged an almost telepathic strike partnership with Kevin Keegan, later went on to enjoy a successful managerial career including spells in charge of football behemoth Real Madrid. But he memorably stated that no manager can influence that link between players and paying punters.

"I don't like champagne, I don't smoke cigars, I haven't any real jewellery at all, apart from the eight pieces of gold I picked up at Anfield," he once said. "The most important relationship at a football club is not between the manager and the chairman, but the players and the fans."

At many clubs, former players who return with their new teams are roundly jeered. Liverpudlians have historically showed more respect. It may be a hackneyed phrase that Liverpool fans are among the most knowledgeable in the game but, as another saying goes, it is only a cliché because it's true.

When Ray Clemence returned with Tottenham in May 1982 after 665 games in 14 years with the Reds, he received a rapturous ovation. Liverpool were closing in on a 13th league title but trailed 1-0 at half-time to a Glenn Hoddle goal. Despite the game being in the balance, Clemence was applauded by the whole crowd as he ran towards the Kop for the start of the second half. He says the memory will never leave him. "The first half I was playing at the Anfield Road end and they were still chanting: 'England's number one' to me so that was nice. I could never have envisaged when I came out at half-time and ran down to the Kop, the reception I would get. The whole stadium stood up and every single one in the Kop. It's probably the most emotional I have ever been at a football ground. It definitely brought a lump to my throat because I could not believe the reception from them. It was just one of the best moments you could possibly have."

Given Liverpool's rivalry with Everton, matches against the Blues have always produced strong emotions. In the earlier encounters between the two this was even more pronounced, particularly as as a number of club officials retained memories of when Anfield was home to Everton.

Prolific Blues striker Dixie Dean gave as good as he got. During the 1927/28 season that saw him achieve the astonishing feat of scoring 60 league goals, he helped himself to a hat trick at Anfield, netting the treble past his great friend Elisha Scott. It's not often that Anfield is silenced but it was on this occasion. "There was nothing quite like quietening the Kop," Dean said years later. "When you stuck a goal in there it all went quiet apart from a bit of choice language aimed in your direction! Scoring there was a delight to me. I just used to turn round to the crowd and bow three times. I had some great fun, though, with the lot of them."

Anfield in full voice though has had an intimidating effect down the years, especially on European nights and, speaking during his last season at the club, Steven Gerrard explained why he'll forever hold the Liverpool crowd in such high esteem. "Had it not been for the backing we received in games both home and on the road en route to Istanbul and then Athens [in 2007], I don't think we'd have got anywhere near the Champions League final on each occasion," he said. "The fans are our twelfth man and when they are charged up, opponents can't deal with it. I've seen some excellent teams freeze and players make decisions they wouldn't normally because of the noise. It's such a massive advantage and I can't emphasize enough how much I appreciate it as captain."

As Liverpool had swept all before them during the 1960s, 70s and 80s, the Reds had made good on Bill Shankly's wish to make Anfield a fortress and a bastion of invincibility. The Kop struck fear into the opposition and many surrendered before the game began. Fast forward to the victorious Champions League campaign of 2004/05 and Anfield still had this amazing aura about it. After seeing his Juventus side beaten 2-1 at Anfield in the quarter-final first leg, Fabio Capello, a manager who'd seen it all during the course of an illustrious career, admitted: "The fantastic atmosphere at Anfield was like an

> *"When the ball was up the other end of the pitch I couldn't help but look up in amazement as the crowd. The whole stadium seemed to be moving, even the people in the stands. They were bobbing up and down, swaying and bouncing. You couldn't better that night."*
> Phil Neal

electric shock for Liverpool's players, who started the match at an astonishing tempo. They seemed unstoppable. At Anfield, even experienced players can have a bad start because of the excitement of playing in such a stadium." A month later, after the semi-final, members of the defeated Chelsea team also admitted to having been affected by the volume of support for the hosts. "The Liverpool fans were amazing that day," said John Terry. "I have never heard anything like it before and I don't think I ever will again. I walked out into that cauldron and heard that singing and saw that passion. The hairs on my arms were standing up.

Of course, that was just one of many memorable European nights under the lights at Anfield. The special atmosphere dates back to the club's very first season in the European Cup and another semi-final when the Reds' twelfth man was worth a goal start.

That legendary night against Helenio Herrera's famous Inter Milan is covered in more detail on page 123 but another famous European occasion to rival either of the aforementioned came in 1977 when French champions St Etienne felt the full force of the red-hot Anfield atmosphere.

Bob Paisley's Reds were closing in on a first European Cup triumph and with a one goal quarter-final first leg deficit to overturn the fans more than played their part. Phil Neal was playing right back for Liverpool on the night and he recalls: "It was the only game in which I found it difficult to focus solely on the football. When the ball was up the other end of the pitch I couldn't help but look up in amazement as the crowd. The whole stadium seemed to be moving, even the people in the stands. They were bobbing up and down, swaying and bouncing, You couldn't better that night." With just six minutes remaining Liverpool led 2-1 but looked to be heading out on the away goals rule. That was until David Fairclough entered the fray and secured a permanent place in Kop folklore by

netting one of the most priceless goals ever scored at Anfield. "The amazing thing is, it seemed so quiet as I homed in on the target but when the ball hit the back of the net the noise was just unbelievable," remembers Fairclough.

That intoxicating environment has had a big impact on opponents with many going on record to speak about the Anfield atmosphere in evangelical terms. A quote from one of the greats of the game, Johan Cruyff, adorns a wall at the Reds' Melwood training base.

Credited with FC Barcelona's modern-day footballing philosophy, the gifted Dutchman said: "There's not one club in Europe with an anthem like 'You'll Never Walk Alone'. There's not one club in the world so united with the fans. I sat there watching the Liverpool fans and they sent shivers down my spine. A mass of 40,000 people became one force behind their team. That's something not many teams have. For that I admire Liverpool more than anything."

One of the game's modern stars, the French forward Thierry Henry, echoed Cruyff's sentiments. "Anfield is the atmosphere I love. It's unbelievable. I've played in a lot of stadiums but for me there is nothing like playing at Liverpool. A kid asked me if I would have liked to play for another team. Straight away I said Liverpool."

Such feelings run deep within the game. During a long managerial career, Harry Redknapp brought West Ham, Portsmouth, Southampton, Tottenham and QPR teams to Anfield. He had been on the wrong end of the Kop's rapier wit in 2012. Two days prior to his acquittal of a tax evasion charge, his Spurs team played out a goalless draw in L4. At one point of the evening, Reds supporters paraphrased the "You're getting sacked in the morning" chant to "You're getting taxed in the morning." Redknapp saw the funny side. During a television interview in April 2015 he was asked if there was one club he would have liked to have taken charge of. "I'd have

> *"There's not one club in Europe with an anthem like 'You'll Never Walk Alone'. There's not one club in the world so united with the fans."*
>
> Johan Cruyff

liked to have managed Liverpool," he responded. "It's a fantastic atmosphere. When that crowd sings 'You'll Never Walk Alone', the hairs stand up on the back of your neck. It's an incredible place and it's a great football club."

The last word goes to Kenny Dalglish, the man who became the King of the Kop after joining from Celtic in 1977. He served Liverpool Football Club with distinction as a player and manager. In the autobiography he penned in 2010, Dalglish paid tribute to the Anfield atmosphere and confessed his one regret. "For all the hundreds of times I performed in front of the Kop, I never

got to stand on it. I never experienced life among that great community nor the surge of emotion as the goalscorer turns to salute them. I wanted to be in among the Liverpool fans, thanking them for being there, for keeping the faith and always reminding the players that, as the anthem says. 'You'll Never Walk Alone'. For those standing on the Kop, I lived a dream they craved. Pulling on the No.7 shirt of Liverpool was an honour I felt hugely yet I envied the fans on the Kop for living the dream I desired. If only I could have joined them to share the atmosphere, jokes, stories and camaraderie. Just once."

Right: Barcelona captain Johan Cruyff leaves the pitch after the Reds had knocked the Catalans out of the 1976 UEFA Cup. Despite the result the Dutch master never forgot his Anfield experience.

"*When we talk about Anfield, it immediately summons up visions of the Kop in full, raucous voice and thrilling football moments.*"

Ian Callaghan

Left: Ian Callaghan played an astonishing 857 games for Liverpool but scored only one hat trick. This goal formed part of that treble against Hull City in December 1973.

Below: David Fairclough scores one of Anfield's most famous goals – the winner against St Etienne in the European Cup quarter-final of 1977 as the Kop roared the Reds to victory.

Opposite top: A Kemlyn Road Stand ticket for that night against St Etienne. Because of the huge crowds outside many ticket holders didn't get in the ground until after the kick-off.

Opposite below: Liverpool fans celebrate "Super Sub's" winner against St Etienne as the Reds take a significant step towards a first European Cup final.

"The amazing thing is, it seemed so quiet as I homed in on the target but when the ball hit the back of the net the noise was just unbelievable."
David Fairclough

Opposite: The King's coronation – Kenny Dalglish runs out of the players' tunnel before his home debut against Newcastle in August 1977. He scored in a 2-0 Liverpool victory.

Above: Kenny grins and bears it on a snowy evening against West Ham United in January 1983. The Reds won 2-1 to book a place in the League Cup semi-finals.

Left: A rosette from the late 1970s featuring an image of Kenny, the new King of the Kop.

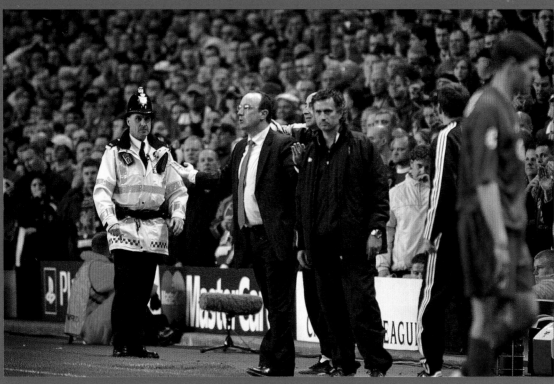

Opposite top: Come on feel the noise! A rousing rendition of "You'll Never Walk Alone" before the memorable Champions League semi-final against Chelsea in 2005.

Opposite below: Rival managers Rafael Benitez and Jose Mourinho patrol the touchline as Anfield becomes gripped by tension during one of the most memorable nights the ground has known.

Above: Five foot seven of football heaven…Liverpool fans hail Luis Garcia after his goal against Chelsea in front of the Kop during that 2005 Champions League semi-final.

" *The Liverpool fans were amazing that day. I have never heard anything like it before and I don't think I ever will again. I walked out into that cauldron and heard that singing and saw that passion. The hairs on my arms were standing up.*"

John Terry, on the 2005 Champions League semi-final

> "To stand on the pitch and look at the Kop when it's full is spectacular. Not just the Kop, but all of Anfield."
>
> Luis Suárez

Above: Returning heroes Luis Suarez and Fernando Torres show their appreciation to Reds supporters following the Liverpool All-Star Charity Match in March 2015.

Left: Fans in the Centenary Stand just can't get enough of Luis Suarez as he celebrates a goal during the 4-0 win over Tottenham in March 2014.

GLORY ROUND THE FIELDS OF ANFIELD ROAD: ANFIELD 1963–1994

CHAPTER SEVEN

GLORY ROUND THE FIELDS OF ANFIELD ROAD: ANFIELD 1963–1994

On the back of Liverpool's long-awaited return to English football's top tier, the directors finally conceded that Anfield was in need of an upgrade. Apart from the installation of floodlights, the ground had remained largely untouched for 35 years.

Now, as a glorious new era dawned, the board signalled their intent on and off the pitch. Years of reluctance to spend big were consigned to the history books. After much haranguing by Bill Shankly and his chief boardroom confidant Eric Sawyer, the purse strings were loosened and Liverpool strode forward, on and off the pitch.

Funds were made available for the manager to strengthen his team and in the same year that the club's transfer record was broken for the second time in three years, a whopping £350,000 – almost

10 times the amount it had cost to sign Peter Thompson – was invested in the construction of Anfield's first new stand for over half a century.

Despite serving the club admirably since being resited and rebuilt in 1906, the old Kemlyn Road stand, with its terraced paddock, had been starting to show its age. For an ambitious club like Liverpool, it seemed out of place in Division One. It was now replaced by a modern cantilever stand that held 6,700 spectators and it meant supporters could no longer move from the Kop to the Anfield Road, and vice-versa, at half-time.

Not since a roof was put over the Kop had Anfield's appearance changed so drastically. Construction began at the tail end of the 1962/63 season, and the final two home games of that campaign were played

Previous pages: Ian St John lets fly with his right foot to open the scoring in a 3-2 victory over Manchester City under the Anfield floodlights in August 1969.

Left: With Stevie Heighway on the wing Liverpool fans had dreams and songs to sing. The Republic of Ireland international is seen here bamboozling Everton's Mick Barnard in an early-1970s Merseyside derby.

Right: Roger Hunt ploughs through the Anfield snow but is unable to prevent the Reds slithering out of the Inter-Cities Fairs Cup against Hungary's Ferencvaros in January 1968.

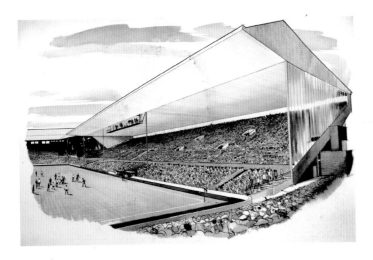

in a ground which housed supporters on just three sides. By the start of the following season the new stand was fully operational, but it proved something of a jinx during the opening months: Liverpool lost their first three games on home soil. "The new stand meant more comfort for the fans but it meant they were further away from the pitch, and the old intimate atmosphere seemed to be lost," remembered Ron Yeats. "This 'new look' Anfield looked different and subconsciously, I think, our players felt as if they were playing on a strange ground."

Liverpool's first season back among the elite resulted in Anfield registering its highest average attendance for over a decade. Although the national trend showed a decrease in crowds at English football grounds, it was boom time at the Kop. With supporters singing along to their Merseybeat favourites and instigating the new phenomenon of terrace chanting, Anfield suddenly found itself at the centre of widespread media attention.

On the afternoon Bill Shankly celebrated his first League title as Liverpool manager, the BBC's popular current affairs show *Panorama* sent a camera crew along to investigate what made the Kop so special. Four months later, on the opening day of the 1964/65 season, the first ever *Match of the Day* was broadcast from Anfield as reigning champions Liverpool played host to Arsenal. "This afternoon we are in Beatleville," explained presenter Kenneth Wolstenholme and so began the longest-running football show on British television. The BBC cameras were back at Anfield in November 1969 to film the first ever colour *Match of the Day*, while in February 1967 40,000 fans watched live coverage of an FA Cup fifth-round tie away to Everton on four specially erected big screens at Anfield.

These were halcyon days at Anfield. Not only were two league titles clinched in front of an exuberant Kop between 1964 and 1966, the FA Cup, Liverpool's holy grail, was finally paraded around the ground

after an agonizing 73-year wait. It came out prior to what was the club's first truly great European night against Inter Milan on 4 May 1965 (see page 123).

The advent of continental competition at Anfield in the mid-1960s was to herald the start of a whole new chapter in the club's history. The atmosphere on a European night was different to anything anyone had experienced before, and such was the clamour to see these matches that they were often as incident-packed off the pitch as on it.

At the quarter-final stage of the European Cup in 1965, for example, a severe snowstorm just prior to kick-off against FC Koln forced the game to be postponed when the majority of fans were already inside the ground. This led to a terrifying crush at the Kop turnstiles as the huge crowd attempted to collect a voucher for the rearranged game as they exited the ground. The following year there was more than 200 casualties at the tie with Ajax when supporters spilled on to the side of the pitch to avoid overcrowding in the Kop.

Even though there'd been further redevelopment in 1965, when a new terrace was erected at the Anfield Road end, the ground was packed out most weeks, so the possibility of moving to a bigger home ground became a hot topic of debate. It was prompted by the club's recently appointed secretary Peter Robinson, who argued that Anfield was not big enough and never would be. He advocated the building of a new stadium in Aintree, which could be shared with Everton, adding that better road and rail rinks made it a much more suitable location. This was a proposal that won support from local politicians, including Harold Wilson, MP for Huyton and the then Prime Minister, and Bessie Braddock, MP for Liverpool Exchange. It didn't go down well with either set of supporters, though, nor with manager Bill Shankly, who threatened to resign if it ever became a reality. Not surprisingly, the idea was taken no further.

Above left: An architect's visualization of how the Main Stand would look after its redevelopment in the early 1970s. This drawing dates back to 1970 and it would be a further three years before the new stand was officially opened.

Above right: Legendary manager Bob Paisley accepts the applause of the Anfield crowd on the occasion of his last home game as Liverpool boss in May 1983. Fittingly he celebrated by lifting the League Championship.

Robinson's idea was certainly ahead of its time because ground-sharing was a subject that would crop up again in later years, but any new stadium would have had to be something special to match the atmosphere generated at Anfield. Other crowds tried to imitate it, but very few came close.

One of the more unusual match nights at Anfield came in August 1971, when Manchester United played a home game in front of the Kop. Old Trafford had been closed due to crowd trouble the previous season and double winners Arsenal provided the opposition, but it was a game that failed to capture the public's imagination. Three nights earlier a crowd of almost 52,000 had watched Liverpool defeat Wolves, yet only just over half that figure saw United come from behind to beat the Gunners.

Further improvements to the ground took place in the early 1970s, with £600,000 being forked out to refurbish the much-loved but now antiquated Main Stand. This involved an extension to the rear so the height could be increased, and the characteristic old roof was replaced by a much more modern-looking structure. It was officially opened by HRH the Duke of Kent in March 1973 and a month later Anfield was reverberating to the sound of another title celebration. Then it staged its first European final, although a torrential downpour just after kick-off forced the abandonment of the UEFA Cup final first leg against Borussia Monchengladbach.

With these big continental games now the norm, another £100,000 was spent on a new floodlighting system, which made these nights seem even more electric. In 1976 a record European crowd of 55,104 saw the Reds secure a famous aggregate victory over Barcelona. Twelve months later, children bunked off school early and workers feigned illness to make sure they weren't locked out when "Supersub" David Fairclough rocked Anfield to its foundations with a never-to-be-forgotten goal against St Etienne, which enabled Liverpool to progress down the road to a first-ever triumph in the European Cup.

During this decade, hooliganism was a growing threat. Although it was never too prevalent at Anfield, it forced the club to erect perimeter fences on three sides of the ground and a protective shield over the players' tunnel prior to the 1977/78 season. This was Kenny Dalglish's debut campaign at Anfield, and it was a season in which the new King of the Kop graced the hallowed turf for both club and country.

In October 1977, Anfield played host to its first full international fixture for 46 years as Wales and Scotland clashed in a vital World Cup qualifier. Although it was a supposedly neutral venue, Wales were officially the home team. They had chosen to play at Anfield after being banned from staging the game in Cardiff due to trouble at a recent game. Given Liverpool's close proximity to Wales, it seemed the ideal venue but what the Welsh FA hadn't accounted for was a mass invasion from north of the border that wiped out any notion of home advantage.

When the two teams ran out, you'd have been forgiven for thinking Hampden Park had been relocated to L4. With the Tartan Army spread all over the ground, the atmosphere was turbo-charged, akin to the many great European nights that Liverpool have been involved in down the

years. A controversial penalty broke the deadlock before Dalglish, fittingly, sealed victory for the Scots with a glancing header at the Anfield Road end two minutes from time.

It was in the red of Liverpool, though, that Dalglish enjoyed greater glory and as the club continued to conquer all before them Anfield became one of the most famous grounds in Europe. Further expansion was delayed by the lengthy process of buying up all the houses behind Kemlyn Road, so in an attempt to provide more seated accommodation for home supporters the Paddock and Anfield Road were both converted from terracing within a year of each other during the early 1980s. The installation of more seats reduced Anfield's overall capacity to around 45,000, but the recession then started to bite hard on Merseyside and unemployment figures hit an all-time high. Demand for tickets dipped and very rarely was the "sold-out" sign required during this period.

It was only when Dalglish, now player/manager, had assembled one of the most exciting teams in Liverpool's history that long queues began to form at the turnstiles again. The Reds, inspired by John Barnes and Peter Beardsley, made a blistering start to the 1987/88 season, but home fans were denied the chance of seeing them in action due to a collapsed Victorian sewer underneath the Kop. Upon further investigation, it was revealed that the problem stemmed from way back in 1906 when the original Kop had been first constructed. Anfield's first three fixtures were postponed, but at least the problem had been detected and a major disaster averted.

Sadly the same could not be said two years later when 96 Liverpool supporters never returned from the FA Cup semi-final against Nottingham Forest at Hillsborough. This was the worst sporting tragedy

in British history and as the city entered a period of mourning, Anfield quickly became a shrine to the victims. Within days, a blanket of flowers covered half the pitch while thousands of scarves were tied to barriers on the Kop and the gates outside. The tributes came from all over the world, creating both a beautiful and moving sight. When football eventually resumed and the inquests began, several short-term measures were immediately put in place to make Anfield a much safer environment, including the removal of the railings at the front of the Kop and a reduction in the capacity of the terrace.

The next changes to the ground came when an upper tier was added to the Kemlyn Road in 1992. To commemorate the club's first century, it was aptly renamed the Centenary Stand and officially opened by UEFA President Lennart Johannson – a hundred years to the day since Liverpool had played its inaugural fixture. The first executive boxes were also installed on that side of the ground as Anfield set about trying to keep pace with the ever increasing commercialization of the game by seeking new ways to increase match-day revenue.

In light of the Hillsborough disaster, spectator safety was now of paramount concern and on the recommendation of the Taylor Report the club announced that Anfield was to become an all-seater stadium. That meant tearing down the iconic Spion Kop, the terrace on which the majority of Liverpudlians had stood since 1906. This was the part of the ground that had come to embody the true spirit of Liverpool Football Club, but Anfield had to move with these changing times. In May 1994 the bulldozers moved in and football's most famous bank of terracing was consigned to the history books.

GREAT GAME
Inter Milan, European Cup semi-final 1st leg
4 May 1965

Anfield's first big European occasion will forever be ranked as its greatest by older supporters. The visit of the reigning world club champions was the cause of much excitement, and lengthy queues snaked their way around the ground from midday.

The red half of Merseyside was already in a state of euphoria following the club's first-ever FA Cup triumph just three days earlier, and an exuberant crowd frightened the life out of the Italians.

The tone for an unforgettable evening was set when Bill Shankly sent out injured stars Gerry Byrne and Gordon Milne with the FA Cup. Liverpool then proceeded to hand out a footballing lesson to Inter's world-famous stars.

Reykjavik, Anderlecht and Cologne had been defeated in the earlier rounds of Liverpool's inaugural campaign of continental competition, and come the end of this night the Reds seemingly had one foot in the final.

By half-time they were 2–1 ahead through goals from Roger Hunt and Ian Callaghan. Sandro

Mazzola's away goal would ultimately prove crucial in the tie, but it failed to dampen the party atmosphere.

Inter's fate could have been worse had a Chris Lawler goal not been disallowed, but Ian St John increased the margin of victory with a goal late in the second half. The home supporters revelled in what they were witnessing and to the tune of 'Santa Lucia' they serenaded the forlorn foreigners with a chorus of "Go Back to Italy". Legendary Inter coach Helenio Herrera later admitted: "We have been beat before but never defeated."

When the final whistle sounded, the entire ground rose as one to acclaim 11 heroes in Red. A controversial 3-0 defeat in Milan a fortnight later ultimately shattered Liverpool's dream of becoming the first British team to reach the European Cup final, but it failed to tarnish the memory of a night that was the standard-bearer for all the great European occasions that followed.

Below: Roger Hunt slams in the opener as Liverpool defeat the reigning world club champions Inter Milan in the first leg of the European Cup in May 1965.

Below right: A rare match ticket for an occasion that is still genuinely regarded as one of Anfield's greatest ever nights.

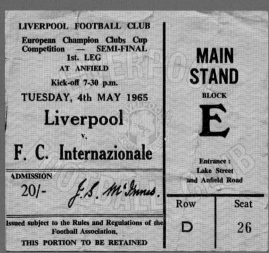

LIVERPOOL FOOTBALL CLUB
European Champion Clubs Cup
Competition — SEMI-FINAL
1st. LEG
AT ANFIELD
Kick-off 7-30 p.m.
TUESDAY, 4th MAY 1965
Liverpool
v.
F. C. Internazionale
ADMISSION
20/-   J.S. McInnes

Issued subject to the Rules and Regulations of the
Football Association,
THIS PORTION TO BE RETAINED

MAIN STAND
BLOCK
E
Entrance :
Lake Street
and Anfield Road

Row | Seat
D | 26

Anfield's new 7,600 seater stand

An artist's impression of Liverpool's new £100,000 Kemlyn Road stand, shows what a spectacular and impressive affair it will be, completely devoid of sight-obstructing supports. Since the announcement in the Daily Post that this stand will be erected in time for the opening of the season, applications for stand season tickets have been coming in daily, to add to the formidable list of applicants, who could not be satisfied at the opening of this season. The continued icy weather is causing some concern, for if the season is extended, as seems certain, the time available for the building of the stand will be cut to disturbing limits. Because of Cup-tie responsibilities to visiting clubs, one quarter of the 7,600 seats cannot be allocated for season ticket purposes.

Opposite top: An artists' impression of the new stand that was built on the Kemlyn Road side of the ground in 1963.

Opposite: Work begins on what was the first new build at Anfield since 1906.

Above: The Kemlyn Road stand was completed in time for the start of the 1963/64 title-winning campaign but proved something of a jinx at first with Liverpool not winning at home until the fourth time of asking.

" *The new stand meant more comfort for the fans but it meant they were further away from the pitch, and the old intimate atmosphere seemed to be lost.*"

Ron Yeats

Above: Bill Shankly conducts the championship celebrations alongside his players from the front row of the directors' box.

Left: The manager proudly poses with his "bread and butter", the League Championship, which he won in 1964, 1966 and 1973.

Opposite: A new roof for the Kop. The cover of football's most famous terrace is stripped to the girders in August 1966 as work takes place to ensure Kopites are kept dry.

"This afternoon we are in Beatleville."

Kenneth Wolstenholme on the first-ever *Match of the Day*

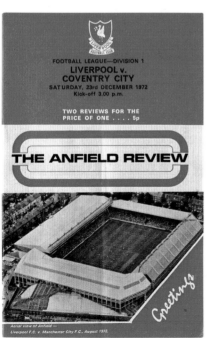

FOOTBALL LEAGUE—DIVISION 1
**LIVERPOOL v.
COVENTRY CITY**
SATURDAY, 23rd DECEMBER 1972
Kick-off 3.00 p.m.

TWO REVIEWS FOR THE
PRICE OF ONE 5p

THE ANFIELD REVIEW

Greetings

Aerial view of Anfield —
Liverpool F.C. v. Manchester City F.C., August 1972.

"The most important relationship at a football club is not between the manager and the chairman, but the players and the fans."

John Toshack

Above: Against the backdrop of Anfield's redeveloped Main Stand John Toshack leaps highest and powers a header towards goal as Southampton are beaten 1-0 in September 1971.

Left: An aerial view of Anfield, complete with new Main Stand, as featured on the front of this match programme from the 1972/73 season.

Opposite: Amid the glare of Anfield's new £100,000 floodlights Phil Boersma challenges for the ball during a 1-0 win over West Ham United in November 1971.

"*When the Kop start singing 'You'll Never Walk Alone' my eyes start to water. There have been times when I've actually been crying while I've been playing.*"

Kevin Keegan

Opposite: Supporters on the Kop pay tribute to their hero Bill Shankly just a few days after the great man passed away in September 1981.

Above: The Anfield flag flies at half-mast as a mark of respect for legendary boss Bill Shankly in the immediate aftermath of his death in 1981.

Right: Going back to their roots. Boyhood Kopites Phil Thompson (4) and Sammy Lee (8) show off the League Championship trophy after a 4-1 home win against Aston Villa in May 1980.

Opposite: In the immediate aftermath of the Hillsborough disaster supporters headed to Anfield to pay their respects, with many tying scarves to the Shankly Gates.

Above: Anfield became a shrine to those who lost their lives at Hillsborough and the pitch was quickly covered with a sea of floral tributes.

Right: 5 May 1990. Anfield hails the last title-winning Liverpool team. From left to right – Grobbelaar, Ablett, Rosenthal, Houghton (partly hidden), Rush, Barnes, Staunton, Hysen and McMahon accept the applause.

THE KOP'S LAST STAND

On the afternoon of Saturday 30 April 1994, Kopites wept as they said goodbye to a dear old friend for the final time. After 88 years, the book was closed on the story of football's most famous terrace.

It was Liverpool's last home game of the season and Norwich City were the visitors. In terms of league positions, the game didn't matter. It had been a campaign to forget for both the players and supporters. A turbulent nine months had witnessed humiliating cup exits and a change of manager. The club was in transition – and so too was Anfield.

To comply with the Taylor Report, the Spion Kop was to be demolished in readiness for the construction of a new, all-seater grandstand. This was the final chance for Kopites to cheer on their team from the terrace that generations had called home since 1906.

It was a deeply moving occasion, one that evoked contrasting emotions. While filled with deep sadness, Anfield was also engulfed by an air of celebration. A pre-match parade of greats from yesteryear got the ball rolling, with all the famous old banners on display behind the goal to greet them. The Kop was at its colourful best and in fine voice.

On the pitch a Jeremy Goss goal condemned the Reds to defeat, but the singing never stopped. When the game was over, the players unveiled a banner thanking Kopites for the unwavering support they had given the team through the years. Afterwards, the supporters refused to go home, staying behind to savour every last remaining minute on the Kop. The legendary terrace had been given the send-off it deserved, and there wasn't a dry eye in the house.

Left: The players salute the standing Kop for the final time on an afternoon when Liverpool slumped to a lacklustre 1-0 defeat against Norwich City.

Right: Reduced to rubble. The once mighty Spion Kop terrace is no more as the bulldozers move in to clear the way for a new all-seater grandstand.

WE ALL LIVE IN A RED & WHITE KOP: THE ARCHITECTURE OF ANFIELD

CHAPTER EIGHT

WE ALL LIVE IN A RED & WHITE KOP: THE ARCHITECTURE OF ANFIELD

Many modern football grounds feel like clones of one another. Out-of-town identikit stadiums-by-numbers that lack soul and make the match-day experience somewhat empty. Not Anfield.

There is no place like home and the nooks and crannies of the famous stadium are crammed full of features that have helped it become a much-loved gem for generations of Liverpudlians.

Every supporter's match day at Anfield starts with the walk to the ground. This will take many different directions: through Stanley Park; up Utting Avenue; along Oakfield, Walton Breck or Back Rockfield Road. Whether fans have parked up in their usual "spec" or travelled by public transport, that walk always provides that special moment when the outline of the grandstands hovers into view. Those coming down Anfield Road will also

pass an imposing red-brick building named Stanley House. This is a symbolic landmark as in the late 1800s the property was owned by John Houlding, Liverpool's future founder.

Houlding, a brewer, would have approved of the fact that an essential part of the game-day routine for many Reds is the pre-match pint. Most of the hostelries around the ground pre-date the club itself having been built in the second half of the 19th century and many represent fine examples of the architecture en vogue at the time. Brewers seized upon triangular corner plots that afforded the design advantage of multiple entrances. The bigger public houses of the day were ostentatious affairs with the bar rooms seeking to offer a homely sanctuary. Meanwhile, the exteriors utilized bright colours in terracotta and glazed

Pevious pages: Touching the famous "This Is Anfield" sign for luck has become a pre-match ritual for every Liverpool player since it was first put up in the early 1970s.

Left: The Shankly Gates were erected in honour of the club's legendary former manager. They were officially opened by his widow Nessie in 1982 and the team has driven through them on a match day ever since.

Right: The Boot Room brains trust. It was in this converted cubby-hole that Messrs Moran, Paisley, Fagan, Evans, Saunders and Bennison plotted the downfall of Liverpool's opponents.

brick with the hoped-for effect of drawing folk to sample the delights within.

Today, popular places for those pre-match tipples and post-match analysis include the Twelfth Man, the Albert, the Park, the King Harry Hotel, the Flat Iron, the Cabbage Hall, the Stanley and the Breck. Their presence also helps explain the history and development of the neighbourhood's landscape. The Twelfth Man was originally called the Salisbury – the same title as another pub slightly further away from the stadium. Both were named after Robert Gascoyne-Cecil, 3rd Marquess of Salisbury and Conservative Prime Minister for three terms between 1885 and 1902. Gascoyne-Cecil's family owned a series of fields stretching from Walton Breck Road to Breckfield Road North.

With thirsts quenched, one of the first landmarks at the stadium itself is what is popularly known as flagpole corner. A poplar meeting place outside the Spion Kop near the junction of Walton Breck Road and what used to be Kemlyn Road, it is home to the top mast of the SS *Great Eastern*, the massive iron sailing ship built by Isambard Kingdom Brunel in the 1850s. The mast had been salvaged when the vessel was broken up and floated up the Mersey. Having been carried by horse to Anfield it had been first raised inside the corner of the outer wall on Oakfield Road in 1891. It is believed that John Houlding and the Everton officials of the day had wanted to erect the mast at the ground as a nod to the city's great connection with the sea and seafaring. It has remained outside the Kop to this day.

At opposite ends of Anfield visitors pass through two grand entrances – sets of gates installed to mark the achievements of a couple of the Reds' legendary managers, Bill Shankly and Bob Paisley.

On Walton Breck Road stands the Paisley Gateway, opened in April 1999 outside the Kop. Bob's widow, Jessie, took an instrumental role in the design of the gates in tandem with architects Atherden Fuller Leng. Jessie was the guest of honour, uncovering the gates to a wide and appreciative audience. Standing at an imposing four-and-a-half metres in height and weighing in at over two tons, the foundations beneath had to be specially strengthened to hold them in place. Prominent in the design of the gates is the European Cup, appearing in three places across the top archway, one for each of Bob's triumphs in Rome, London and Paris. The gates themselves feature the crests of Bob's birthplace, Hetton-le-Hole, and the Liver Bird of his "adopted" city of Liverpool. The Hetton-le-Hole crest is made up of an eye-catching early steam engine, an acknowledgement of the area's pioneering role in the rail revolution. Four footballs surround each of the crests. On the brick pillars flanking the gates sit two bronze reliefs, one depicting the man himself and the other detailing the list of honours he brought to Liverpool Football Club.

Opened 17 years earlier on Anfield Road are the Shankly Gates, which were unveiled by Bill's widow Nessie. With the words "You'll Never Walk Alone" emblazoned across the 20-foot-wide overthrow, they also feature a heraldic symbol showing the Liver Bird, the Cross of St Andrew and a thistle to denote Bill's Scottish origins.

Somerset blacksmith and Reds fan, Ken Hall, was the man who made the gates in just 10 weeks. Speaking to the club's official magazine in 2014, he recalled: "Our design was one of ten which had been originally submitted and Mrs Shankly picked ours – she said there was nothing to touch

it. My colleague Chris Brooks worked on the overthrow and I forged the gates themselves. We were shattered at the end but always confident about completing them on time. Enthusiasm got us through – it was definitely a labour of love."

Shankly's contribution in revolutionizing the Reds from a team struggling to get out of the Second Division to a football force admired across the globe is also recognized in the shape of a statue. The bronze cast of the great man, arms aloft and with a Liverpool scarf around his neck, was unveiled outside the Kop in 1997.

The four-sided plinth, naturally made from Scots granite, is inscribed with the words: "Bill Shankly – he made the people happy." Standing at over eight feet high, it was crafted by Liverpool artist Tom Murphy, who studied video footage and photographs as well as seeking input from Nessie, ex-Liverpool players, and even Bill's former tailor before starting work on the sculpture which weighs in at three-quarters of a ton. It was commissioned and financed by then club sponsors, Carlsberg. Murphy explained: "I wanted to make the statue look like a living thing. The pose I chose is one people will immediately recognize – arms straight out and triumphant, saluting victory before his adoring fans." The statue is now a popular place to meet before the match and the venue for millions of selfies!

Located just behind the Shankly statue is the club's Museum, which was relaunched midway through the 2013/14 season. The interactive Liverpool Story was officially opened by manager Brendan Rodgers. He unveiled a plaque to mark the moment and said:

"This club has an incredible history and to see it all housed in one place is brilliant. Fans from across the world can enjoy the real history of their club in a new and exciting way." Every visitor is now provided with a multimedia handset offering a 40-minute commentary by Phil Thompson, who shares his experiences of being a fan, player, captain, assistant manager and manager. There's also a chance to see the club's European trophies and have a picture taken in the state-of-the-art photo booth with a choice of iconic LFC images. The plaque unveiled by Rodgers isn't the only one housed in the Museum's headquarters. The Kop entrance also includes one to the memory of the great Liverpool player Billy Liddell, which was revealed in 2004.

In addition to the myriad of features marking some of the Reds' happiest moments, the outside of the stadium also offers fitting tributes to the club's darkest days.

The Hillsborough Memorial is the most sacred part of Anfield. Former Liverpool captain Jamie Redknapp played in the Celebration of the 96 match which marked the 25th anniversary of the disaster. Ahead of that game, he recalled his early days at the club: "I stayed in digs for about three years and the Eternal Flame was right by me. Along with attending the memorial service every year, I'd walk into the ground every day and see the flame and just have a little look. You only then realize the magnitude of it." Design proposals for the redevelopment of the Main Stand include a colonnade that will become the new home for the memorial. While building work takes place

during 2015 and 2016 a specially commissioned temporary memorial – designed with input from the families – was put in place by the Centenary Stand. Just yards away from it is a plaque which stands as a permanent tribute to the 39 football fans who died at the 1985 European Cup final. Ex-Reds defender Phil Neal and former Juventus player Sergio Brio unveiled the plaque at a special ceremony held in 2010.

With so many storied teams, great players and pioneering managers, Anfield has become a sacred place for many fans all over the world. Thousands make a special pilgrimage every year to see the club's famous home and an essential part of their journey is a tour that takes them inside one of the great cathedrals of football. Inside the front doors, an essential stop-off point is the old Boot Room, nowadays used as a base for journalists before domestic fixtures and for managers to hold their post-match press conferences. It is forever associated with an Anfield dynasty founded by Bill Shankly and where Liverpool FC's finest hours were plotted.

As it happens, Shanks was anything but a Boot Room man. Reliable sources suggest that he would mainly venture in to offer coach Reuben Bennett a lift home after training. "Occasionally he'd show his face," recalled Roy Evans, one of his disciples and a future Reds boss himself. "But it was Bob [Paisley], Joe [Fagan] and Ronnie [Moran] – they started that side of it, it was their domain. We were there every day. We used to come in on Sundays regularly, from 10 to 12. It was nothing fancy, just a little room that we had to hang our coats and chat about football over a cup of tea or sometimes a beer." It was strictly private, although opposition managers were always welcome for a post-match drink. Even

the players were prohibited. Any caught loitering outside suffered the wrath of Moran.

There was, of course, a great mythology that grew about the Boot Room but it was all opium for the Kop's masses. While fans could only begin to imagine what secrets were shared in this most mysterious of meeting rooms, the select few who gained access described a shabby room 12ft by 12ft reeking of dubbin and liniment; its floor space occupied by tatty kit hampers or beer crates which doubled up as seats; its walls plastered with faded photographs and calendars and cupboards stacked with notepads, *Rothmans Football Yearbook*s and drinks. Like its patrons, it was deliberately unremarkable. Its demolition in 1993 was seen as an outrage but was a step taken out of purely practical necessity.

A look around the inner sanctum also calls for a stop-off at the home dressing room – the four walls inside which many a motivational talk from the club's great managers has been delivered. It is mind-blowing to think that this is the place where so many Liverpool greats prepared for many a triumph in the all-red kit.

Once through the door, however, the reaction of most visitors is a kind of inverse-Tardis response – "it's smaller on the inside". Not much has changed in the past 25 years and the opposition dressing room is actually more spacious. But the level of intimacy has helped forge a great team spirit down the years and, as the old adage goes, if it ain't broke why fix it?

Stepping out of the dressing room and into the tunnel, you are met by the This is Anfield sign at the top of the steps that descend on to the pitch – surely the most famous piece of wall art in any players' tunnel? Bill Shankly had introduced the sign in 1974

Above: Thanks to supporter groups such as "Spion Kop 1906" Anfield is awash with colour before every home game and the atmosphere these banners help generate is the envy of grounds across the country.

Right: The seven-foot tall bronze statue of Bill Shankly that stands outside the Kop. It was created by sculptor Tom Murphy and unveiled in 1997.

> *"I wanted to make the statue look like a living thing. The pose I chose is one people will immediately recognize – arms straight out and triumphant, saluting victory before his adoring fans."*
>
> **Tom Murphy on his Bill Shankly statue**

as a psychological ploy designed to strike fear into opponents as they prepared to take on the Reds. In his own words, Shankly saw it as a way of reminding "our lads who they're playing for and to remind the opposition who they're playing against".

The sign, traditionally touched by Liverpool players as they make their way into the arena, was replaced with an updated version in 1998 but the original was restored in July 2012 by new manager Brendan Rodgers. "When you come into a football club you need to have a real sense of the past, a sense of the present and a sense of the future," he explained. "I just felt that this was a sign and a symbol of what Liverpool was for many years. For me it's a mark of the Anfield of old. We're very much in the modern era but I think it's very important to remember the great past of this football club and the This is Anfield sign is a massive part of that. There's no doubt that Anfield is one of the most celebrated and historic venues in world football. So to put up the sign was just another little element of trying to restore the great days here."

Once down the tunnel and outside, a quick glance to the right and you are met by one of the most magnificent sights in football: the Kop. The history of that end of the stadium is covered in other chapters but its importance to the Liverpool story cannot be overestimated. "The Spion Kop at Liverpool is an institution," declared Shankly. "And if you're a member of the Kop you feel as if you're a member of a big society, where you've got thousands of friends all round about you. And they're united and loyal." The modern-day Kop is the biggest single-tier stand in England, with 76 rows of seats accommodating 12,409 spectators.

The technical area used by the management teams is also unusual. Along with their backroom staff and substitutes, the bosses currently watch the action from seats that make up part of the Paddock. This was brought into effect when the old brick dug-outs, hand-built by Bob Paisley in the 1950s, were replaced in 1993. The two teams sit directly next to each other with no partition between them and the seats are not located directly on the halfway line due to the location of the players' tunnel.

Sharp-eyed spectators will also note another unique feature in the very goals themselves – red nets. Goal nets were invented for football in 1889 by a Liverpool civil engineer, John Brodie, the man who also designed the first Mersey road tunnel in 1934. Red nets had been a feature at the stadium since the late 1960s and like the This is Anfield sign before it, were reintroduced at the request of Brendan Rodgers in 2012 after he had been given a private tour of the ground soon after being named manager. It is thought they were in place between 1968 and 1995 with club museum curator Stephen Done revealing: "Some of Roy Evans's players claimed they could not see the red-netted goal against the backdrop of the Kop, so the nets were duly changed. The players might have had a point, but it never seemed to be a problem for the likes of Ian Rush, John Barnes and John Aldridge – let alone Roger Hunt! Brendan and his family were given their first glimpse of Anfield the day after he was unveiled as manager. At the end of the tour we stood on the Kop and Brendan commented that he always remembered the goals at Anfield having red nets. He suggested we bring them back."

Liverpool Football Club is therefore privileged to have an extraordinary home that is packed full of character, the details of which – along with its sights, shapes, smells and sounds – contribute to the very particular Anfield aesthetic.

"*The Spion Kop at Liverpool is an institution. And if you're a member of the Kop you feel as if you're a member of a big society, where you've got thousands of friends all round about you. And they're united and loyal.*"

Bill Shankly

Above: One of the last photographs taken of the old terraced Kop; taken in the spring of 1994, shortly before it made way for a new all-seated grandstand.

Opposite: Despite all the redevelopment work at Anfield through the years, the top mast from Brunel's SS *Great Eastern* has remained in the exact same spot since 1891.

Opposite: The legendary sign that greets the players as they make their way out on to the Anfield pitch. It's said to strike fear into the opposition and inspire those in red.

Top: Take a walk up Walton Breck Road from the direction of Everton Valley and before reaching the Spion Kop you'll come across the famous Albert pub where many Liverpool songs have been written.

Above left: A pin badge from the 1980s bearing the unofficial Liverpool motto and the title of a song you'll hear played at Anfield before every match.

Above right: Supporters hang around outside the old standing Kop on the afternoon of its last stand in April 1994.

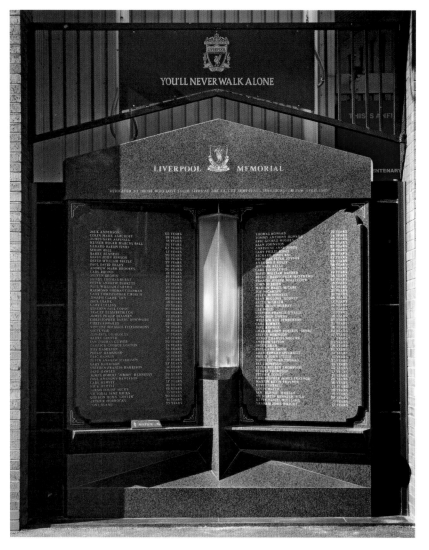

> **" Along with attending the memorial service every year, I'd walk into the ground every day and see the flame and just have a little look. You only then realize the magnitude of it."**
> **Jamie Redknapp**

Top: The "Paisley Gateway" under construction. A prominent feature in the design is the three European Cups Bob won as Liverpool manager.

Left: Anfield's memorial to the 96 Liverpool supporters who lost their lives at the Hillsborough disaster in Sheffield on 15 April 1989.

Opposite: Unveiled in 1999, the "Paisley Gateway" in front of the Kop is Anfield's tribute to English football's most successful manager.

"It was nothing fancy, just a little room that we had to hang our coats and chat about football over a cup of tea or sometimes a beer."

Roy Evans on the famous Anfield Boot Room

Left: The Boot Room boys pose for a photograph in the old Main Stand Paddock, prior to Bob Paisley's first season as manager in 1974/75. (back row left to right) Saunders, Bennett, Twentyman, Fagan (middle row) Bennison, Moran, Evans (front row) Paisley.

Opposite: The sign that hung on the door of the fabled Anfield Boot Room. What went on beyond that door remains one of the best-kept secrets in football.

Below: A plan of Anfield's inner sanctum, as drawn up by an architect in 1970. This drawing of the Main Stand floor-plan clearly shows where the legendary Boot Room was situated.

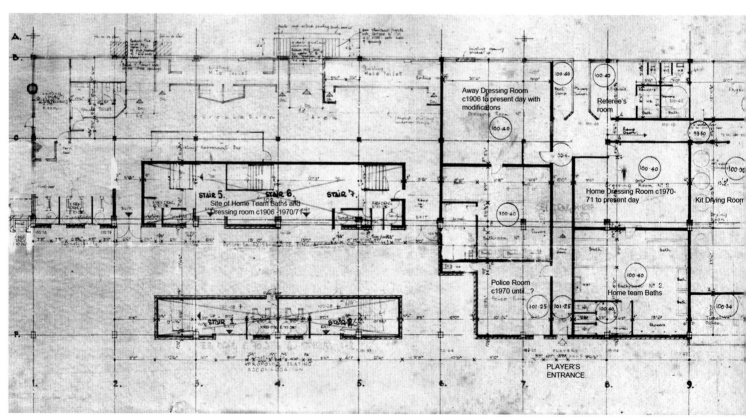

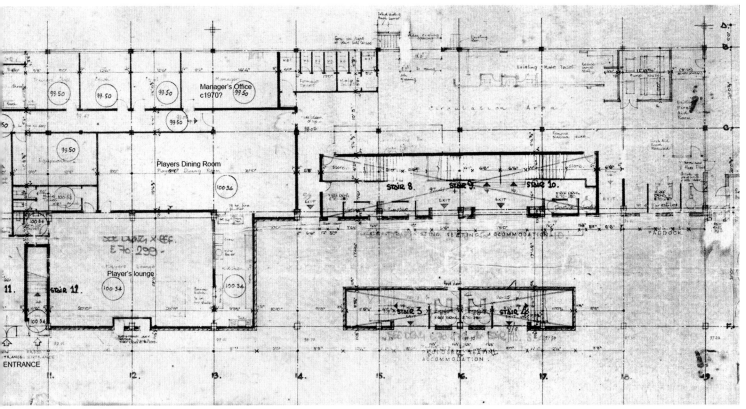

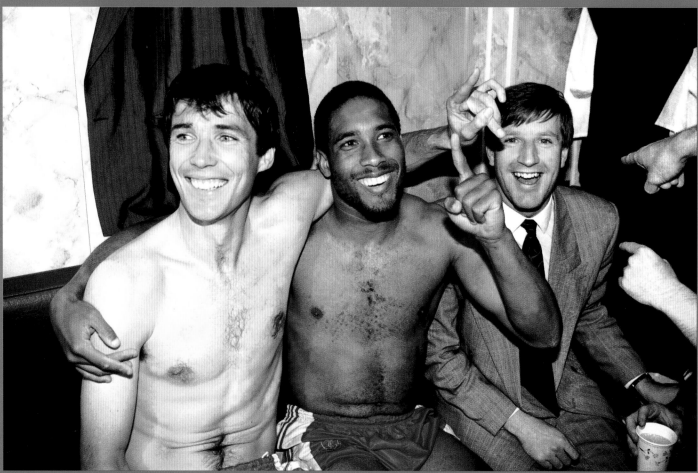

Opposite top: Liverpool's class of '64 toast the club's first league title triumph in 17 years. Note that the dressing room back then was the original one designed by Archibald Leitch in 1906.

Opposite below: Another championship celebration, this time from 1990 and in the dressing room that the players still use today. The team featuring Alan Hansen and John Barnes had just overcome Queens Park Rangers to win their 18th league title.

Below: Did you know that the home team dressing room at Anfield is actually smaller than the away dressing room?

"There's no doubt that Anfield is one of the most celebrated and historic venues in world football."
Brendan Rodgers

INTO THE NEW CENTURY:
ANFIELD 1994–2015

CHAPTER NINE

INTO THE NEW CENTURY: ANFIELD 1994–2015

The 1990s was a period of great change in English football. The growth of satellite TV, the dawn of the Premier League and the introduction of all-seater stadiums combined to radically transform the face of the game in this country.

At Anfield, this new era was officially ushered in when the Kop Grandstand rose from the rubble of the much-loved but now demolished terrace. There had been a minor last-ditch campaign by some supporters to try and prevent the Kop being seated but after what everyone had been through at Hillsborough it was widely accepted that terracing should be consigned to a bygone age.

Liverpool's home ground without its world-renowned standing Kop, however, took some getting used to. The shiny new structure went up in stages during the 1994/95 season and the huge void created a surreal atmosphere. The opening home game of Anfield's first terrace-less campaign saw Robbie Fowler hit the headlines with a famous record-breaking hat trick against Arsenal but with one end of the ground still in the throes of construction it was witnessed by a crowd of only just over 30,000.

With the gradual installation of more seats, attendances rose throughout the season and on the final day 40,014 saw Kop legend Kenny Dalglish celebrate lifting the Premier League title as manager of Blackburn Rovers.

Once completed, the new stand's 12,000 capacity was less than half of what the old terrace once held but it became the largest single-tiered stand in the country and, as would be proved in the coming years, the noise generated could be just as intimidating as the Kop of old.

Despite the dismissive view of some traditionalists, Anfield was certainly moving with the times and its impressive modernization did not go unnoticed. In 1996 it was awarded the honour of being a host venue for Euro '96, the first major

international tournament held in England since the 1966 World Cup. Having been overlooked in favour of Goodison back then, this was just reward for the off-field progress made by the club in the intervening three decades.

As a warm-up for the finals, Anfield also staged a play-off game between the Republic of Ireland and Holland in December 1995 and a fantastic atmosphere that night whetted the appetite for the following summer. Anfield was allocated games in Group B and opened its doors to Italy, Russia and a Czech Republic team featuring future Liverpool stars Patrik Berger and Vladimir Smicer. Three highly entertaining games, that saw 12 goals

Previous pages: All the flags and banners were out in force to give the standing Kop a wonderful send-off when supporters stood on it for the final time on 30 April 1994.

Left: Steven Gerrard places the ball down ready to take a corner at Anfield during a Premier League match against Arsenal, the Kop is in the background with the Main Stand to the right.

Right: A flyer advertising the concert that took place at Anfield the day after the standing Kop's last game. It proved a fitting finale for football's best-loved terrace.

£2.00 Donation

Anfield
Sunday 1st May 1994

"Caring In The Community"

The Last Night of The Kop

A Unique Celebrity Tribute to Football's Musical Legend

BROOKSIDE

Barnardos
Merseyside Centenary Appeal
Registered Charity No. 216250

scored, were watched by a combined crowd of 93,568, while a further 37,465 saw a dour quarter-final tie in which France eventually beat Holland after a penalty shoot-out.

In 1997 an upper tier was added to the Anfield Road, creating room for 2,500 extra seats. Previous attempts to build up this end of the ground had been continually blocked by residents in the houses directly behind the stand but by building it at a reduced height planning permission was finally granted. In May 2000, however, there was cause for concern when incessant bouncing by visiting Celtic fans, who had travelled south in large numbers for Ronnie Moran's testimonial match, caused a slight swaying of the structure. To allay safety fears the club was forced to insert three steel columns to strengthen it ahead of the next campaign.

The following year saw Anfield stage its first full England international for 70 years. With Wembley being rebuilt, the national team's fixtures were played at selected club grounds throughout the country and in a five-year spell between 2001 and 2006 Liverpool hosted three of these games: a World Cup qualifier against Finland and friendlies with Paraguay and Uruguay.

At club level, Anfield had witnessed little in the way of success since the 1980s but the global appeal of the club meant that demand for tickets was increasing all the time. Unfortunately, the ground was not big enough to meet the requests and the already lengthy queue for season tickets was becoming almost unmanageable. When it came to match-day-generated revenue Liverpool were falling behind their main Premier League rivals at a worrying rate, which, in turn, was having a knock-on effect on the manager's spending power in the transfer market.

At the time it was believed that Anfield was unable to be sufficiently expanded so this led to renewed calls for the club to explore the option of moving to a new stadium that would provide a much bigger capacity.

In June 2000 it was revealed that the club planned to leave their home of 108 years and build a 60,000-seater stadium on Stanley Park. With the potential to add an extra 10,000 seats at a later date, it was an exciting proposition. Plans were drawn up but less than a year later an alternative site in Speke was being considered due to fears that an inquiry into the planning application would severely delay work on the project.

Above: Supporters refuse to go home as loyal Kopites say their final goodbyes to the terrace on which they had cheered the Reds for so long.

Right: A view from the Anfield Road as Anfield braces itself for another big European night in October 2014. Unfortunately, on this occasion it ended in defeat to Real Madrid.

> *"We've had some of the greatest triumphs in our history here, so it makes sense if there's a right solution that this is the place we should continue to play our football."*
>
> *Ian Ayre, Liverpool Chief Executive Officer*

A move to the outskirts of the city was naturally met with objection from the majority of supporters who believed the club should remain as close to its Anfield roots as possible and, fortunately for them, the idea was soon abandoned. The stadium saga then took another twist when it was announced that Stanley Park was back on the agenda, although rising costs and uncertainty over the ownership of the club saw those plans stall.

Amid all this talk of moving grounds, Liverpool's on-field fortunes picked up, especially in continental competition. Gerard Houllier's cup treble of 2001 started the restoration process before Rafael Benitez picked up the baton and reinforced their credentials. It was during this time that the unique Anfield atmosphere began to reverberate across Europe once again. The Kop was striking fear into the opposition just as it had done before and those electric nights of the past, which were thought to be relics of a glorious bygone age, were joyously rekindled.

In the first decade of the 2000s AS Roma, Barcelona, Olympiacos, Juventus, Chelsea, Inter Milan and Real Madrid all succumbed to the ferocious force of a passionate Anfield crowd, proof, if it was ever needed, that the legendary wall of sound could not be silenced by an all-seater stadium.

Such occasions, notably the semi-final second leg of the never-to-be-forgotten Champions League winning campaign of 2004/05 (see page opposite) strengthened Anfield's reputation as one of the great venues in world football and prompted many supporters to doubt the wisdom of Liverpool ever contemplating a departure from its spiritual home.

By the time Rafa guided the Reds to a second Champions League final in 2007 the club was finally in the hands of new owners, American businessmen Tom Hicks and George Gillett. Their vision included picking up the pieces of the intended move to Stanley Park. Revised plans, produced by architects based in Dallas, were unveiled and part of the park fenced off, ready for work to begin. However, the bold promise made by Hicks and Gillett, to "have a spade in the ground within 60 days" was to come back and haunt them.

During what was one of the most turbulent times in its history, the club staggered from one crisis to another under the ill-fated guidance of the aforementioned owners and, not surprisingly, their grand plans for the proposed new stadium never did materialize.

In 2010, much to the relief of every Liverpudlian, Hicks and Gillett were finally forced to sell up. Boston-based New England Sports Ventures, owned by John W. Henry, took control of the club and littered among

the mess they inherited was the issue of whether to press on with plans to build a new stadium or look into the prospect of redeveloping Anfield.

It was now a ten-year-old problem and despite the best efforts of the team on the pitch, the club was still struggling to keep up with its main competitors on a financial footing. It was clear that it would stay this way until the stadium issue was resolved so, not surprisingly, it was placed high on the list of priorities.

Finally, in October 2012, following an extensive consultation process, it was revealed that, subject to planning permission, Liverpool's preferred option was to stay at Anfield. "We've had some of the greatest triumphs in our history here, so it makes sense if there's a right solution that this is the place we should continue to play our football," said the club's chief executive officer Ian Ayre. It was a decision that delighted the vast majority of the club's ever-broadening fan base.

Two years later, plans for the new 21,000-seater Main Stand were unveiled to the public for the first time. The artist's impressions were met with widespread approval. When completed, the overall capacity of the ground will rise to around 54,000, while outline proposals for a new stand at the Anfield Road end could see an extra 4,800 seats added at a later date. On 4 December 2014, it was officially announced that building work on the expansion of Anfield was about to begin, with Ayre describing it as "a great day for the football club and all its fans."

After over a decade of uncertainty the path was now clear and everyone at Liverpool Football Club could start looking ahead to a bigger and better future.

Above: A cauldron of noise awaits the players of Liverpool and Manchester United as they prepare to do battle in a Premier League fixture at Anfield in October 2009.

GREAT GAME:
Liverpool v Chelsea, Champions League semi-final 2nd leg
3 May 2005

With a place in the Champions League final at stake this was always going to be a unique occasion but even by Anfield's high standards the atmosphere on this night was unprecedented in the modern era.

"When we were warming-up 40 minutes before the game, the crowd was noisy," recalled the club's then vice-captain Jamie Carragher. "Normally you can hear DJ George playing his records, but even he was drowned out by the singing. We knew then it was going to be a special night."

With every single Liverpool fan inside the stadium roaring the Reds on, the Premiership champions-elect buckled. Chelsea boss Jose Mourinho later admitted, "I felt the power of Anfield, it was magnificent," while his players also conceded that they had never experienced anything like it.

From the first whistle to the last, the decibels levels never dipped. It inspired every one of the Liverpool players and they rose to the occasion.

With the tie evenly poised following a goalless draw at Stamford Bridge a week earlier it was a game fraught with tension but the ground erupted after just four minutes when Liverpool controversially took the lead through a goal that will forever spark debate.

It came via the left boot of Luis Garcia. Chelsea claimed the ball didn't cross the line but fortunately the linesman's flag said otherwise. Eidur Gudjohnsen spurned a gilt-edged opportunity to break Liverpudlian hearts in stoppage time before scenes of wild celebration greeted confirmation that Liverpool's ticket to the Ataturk had been booked.

Those who argued that all-seater stadiums could not generate the pulsating atmosphere of old had been proven wrong. This was a night that harked back to the glory days of the standing Kop at its very best. Some even say it was better.

Right: Even the fans in the stands were shouting at the top of their voices and dancing on their seats as Liverpool defeated Chelsea to reach the 2005 Champions League final.

Above: We all live in a green and white Kop. For one night only the Kop was home to Republic of Ireland supporters as their country took on Holland at Anfield in a play-off for Euro 96.

Left: Anfield staged four matches during the 1996 European Championships, including this quarter-final tie between Holland and France that the latter won on penalties.

Opposite: In 1997 building work began on transforming the Anfield Road stand into the double-decker structure that we know today.

> *"Anfield is the atmosphere I love. It's unbelievable. I've played in a lot of stadiums but for me there is nothing like playing at Liverpool."*
>
> **Thierry Henry**

Above: Home and away shirts from the 1995/96 season hang side by side in the Anfield dressing room.

Opposite: Local lad and Liverpool legend Robbie Fowler gets a front-row seat at the Last Night of the Kop concert on 1 May 1994.

Left: Stan Collymore celebrates after scoring a late winner in a thrilling 4-3 victory at home to Newcastle in April 1996. It was a match that ranks as one of the most dramatic ever played at Anfield.

"The fans are our 12th man and when they are charged up, opponents can't deal with it. I've seen some excellent teams freeze and players make decisions they wouldn't normally because of the noise. It's such a massive advantage and I can't emphasize enough how much I appreciate it as captain."
Steven Gerrard

Left: The five silver mini European Cups awarded to Liverpool FC after each of their five cup triumphs by UEFA. They are on display at LFC Museum which is situated behind the Kop.

Opposite top: Anfield on a Champions League night during the unforgettable run to Istanbul in 2004/05. This game against Deportivo La Coruna ended goalless.

Opposite middle: Jubilant supporters scale the gates outside Anfield to welcome home Liverpool's 2005 Champions League-winning heroes.

Opposite below: The atmosphere at Anfield on a big European night is unrivalled. This was the scene prior to the Europa League semi-final tie against Atletico Madrid in 2010.

Left: Beatles legend Paul McCartney rocks the Kop during his Anfield concert in 2008, staged to celebrate the city of Liverpool's status as 'Capital of Culture'.

Below: A spectacular night view from the upper tier of the Anfield Road looking towards the Spion Kop at the start of the game against Aston Villa in December 2010.

"The fantastic atmosphere at Anfield was like an electric shock for Liverpool's players, who started the match at an astonishing tempo. They seemed unstoppable. At Anfield, even experienced players can have a bad start because of the excitement of playing in such a stadium."

Fabio Capello, Juventus manager in 2005

Opposite: One of the stunning gold-coloured Liverbird badges that were attached to the Main Stand entrance gates at the Kop end of the ground.

Above: "We Are Liverpool…tra-la-la-la-la": supporters line the streets of Anfield to give the Reds a rousing reception during the exciting climax to the 2013/14 season.

Left: The Anfield crowd look on as Philippe Coutinho is congratulated after his goal against Manchester City on 1 March 2015.

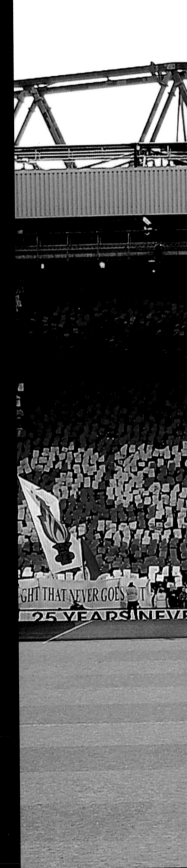

ANFIELD LEGEND
REMEMBERING THE 96

The victims of the Hillsborough disaster will never be forgotten at Anfield.

On 15 April 1989, 24,000 Liverpool supporters travelled to Sheffield to watch their team in the FA Cup semi-final against Nottingham Forest. Ninety-six never returned.

In the immediate aftermath of the disaster, with the city plunged into a deep period of mourning, Anfield became a shrine to their memory and the focal point for a mass outpouring of grief. The pitch was covered in a blanket of flowers, while hundreds of scarves were tied to the goalposts, the barriers on the Kop and the gates outside.

Describing the scenes in his end of season diary, manager Kenny Dalglish, wrote: "It is difficult to explain the atmosphere at Anfield. It was nothing like I had experienced before – a mixture of grief, confusion and calm. All the players were there and we went on to the pitch and saw some fans. No-one was really talking, just nodding, shaking hands. It was quiet, so quiet. The pitch area is normally a cauldron of noise when the fans come face to face with the players, but this wasn't a day for celebrating."

Exactly 12 months on from the day of the tragedy, a permanent memorial, featuring an eternal flame, with the names of all who died etched in the marble, was erected and unveiled at the Main Stand end of Anfield Road by Bill Shankly's widow Nessie.

Each year, on the anniversary of Britain's worst sporting disaster, the doors of Anfield are opened up and supporters take their seats to remember those we lost on that fateful day. The normal big-match atmosphere is replaced by a mood of sombre reflection. A poignant service is conducted and at six minutes past three, a minute's silence observed.

If any good came out of what happened on that never-to-be-forgotten day at Hillsborough it was the improvement in conditions at football grounds across the country. A report by Lord Justice Taylor led to increased safety measures and all-seater stadiums. It was a watershed moment in the history of the sport and Anfield, as much as anywhere else, has fully embraced the changes.

During Anfield's current redevelopment, the Hillsborough Memorial has been placed in safe storage while a specially commissioned temporary memorial can now be seen close to the main entrance of the Centenary Stand.

Collectively, the victims are known as "the 96" and though their lives were prematurely cut short in the most tragic of circumstances their names will live on for ever at Anfield.

Right: A mosaic is displayed by fans on the Kop as the two teams hold a minute's silence in honour of the 25th anniversary of the Hillsborough tragedy before the Barclays Premier League match between Liverpool and Manchester City at Anfield on 13 April 2014.

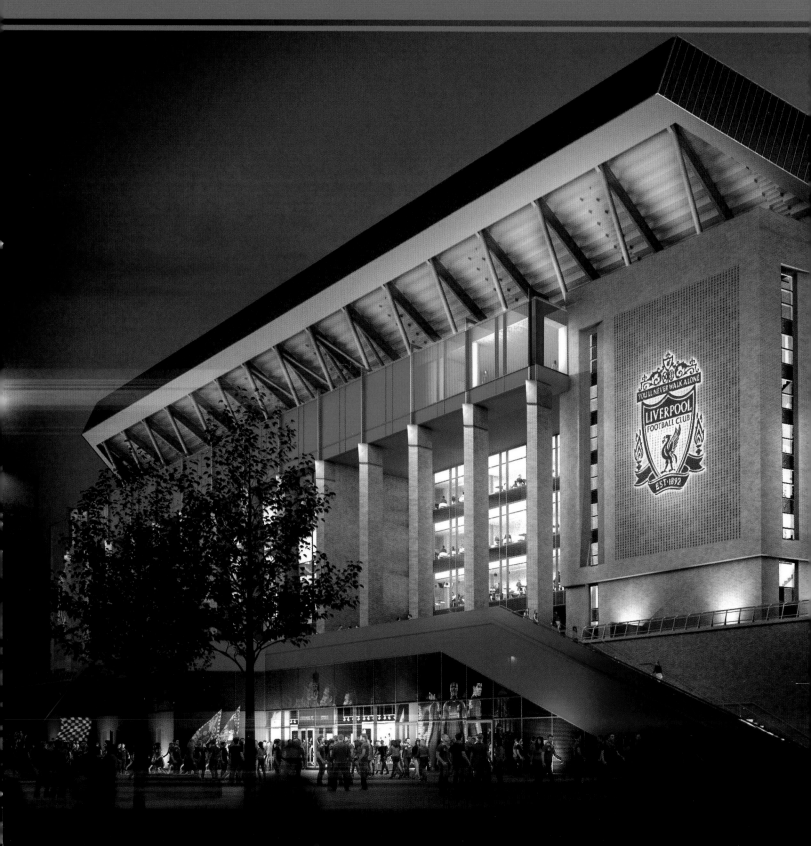

CHANGING ANFIELD: THE FUTURE

CHAPTER TEN

CHANGING ANFIELD: THE FUTURE

Almost 15 years after Liverpool Football Club had revealed plans to move to a new home, building work began on the first phase of a revamped Anfield.

Owners Fenway Sports Group had previously overseen a successful redevelopment of Fenway Park, the historic home of the Boston Red Sox baseball team and after careful consultation with various parties opted to press ahead with a similar option for LFC.

The first stage of work on adding 8,250 seats to the Main Stand – as well as new office and conferencing space – commenced on 8 January 2015 with the intention being that it would be completed in time for the beginning of the 2016/17 season. In a second stage of expansion, additional seating in the Anfield Road stand could be added to give the stadium a total capacity of just over 58,000.

Chairman Tom Werner explained: "Since Fenway Sports Group took ownership of the club, we were committed to explore in depth all options for the future of Anfield Stadium. We listened to fans, the community, partners, the Supporters' Committee and key stakeholders involved in the club. It was just over two years ago that we said our preference was to stay at Anfield and here we are announcing that the expansion is going ahead. We have made more progress in the past two years than in the last decade.

"Having experience of expanding Fenway Park and being through a similar and very successful project for the Red Sox, everyone at FSG is extremely proud and excited to be part of expanding Anfield Stadium. Resolving the stadium issue will be our legacy at Liverpool."

The Reds' chief executive officer Ian Ayre felt that the unveiling of the designs, produced by architects KSS, had represented a key milestone in the long-running saga of the stadium project. "It's a significant step forward," he said. "We set out a very clear set of objectives and timescales to achieve what we want to on the stadium and it's very much on track. Although for the fans it feels like it's been a ten-year or more wait, under this ownership we've been at this in earnest for two to two-and-a-half years and we've made progress in keeping with the plan we set. Staying at Anfield and finding such a great solution is fantastic for everyone. There is still an incredible amount to do, but good progress has been made so far and we are proud to be able to unveil our plans."

Alongside these plans, the club signed a legal agreement with Liverpool City Council and Your Housing Group to regenerate the surrounding Anfield area as part of the stadium renovation scheme. The Anfield Project aims to combine increased employment and training opportunities for local people with a vision for creating an attractive environment for the surrounding community.

Proposals included new and refurbished housing and the development of a public square, to be named "96 Avenue" in honour of the Liverpool supporters who died at Hillsborough. Commercial and retail premises are also planned along the High Street, while a range of developments will complete the restoration of Stanley Park. Anfield Sports and Community Centre will also undergo a redevelopment as part of a £2.3m scheme that will enable the charity to offer improved sporting facilities and programmes to people living in North Liverpool. Working with funding partners including the club, the ASCC's Football 4 Everyone programme will bring much-needed investment to the centre. Major improvements will include a new full-size floodlit artificial grass pitch, a three-court sports hall and the refurbishment of existing artificial pitches. One of the key projects will be the construction of a "Cruyff Court" which will provide youngsters with a safe place to play sports as well as health and personal development support, funded by Dutch football legend Johan Cruyff's Foundation. It will be the third such facility in the UK and the first outside London.

Previous pages: An evocative artist's impression of how Anfield will look under the lights when the Main Stand expansion is completed in the summer of 2016.

Left: The new-look Main Stand will feature an expanded concourse while the structure itself will feature the Reds' famous club crest.

Mayor of Liverpool, Joe Anderson, said: "This is another important step in our ambitions to transform the Anfield area, bringing new jobs, investment and housing. The overall regeneration of Anfield will see £260m invested in the local community and will deliver hundreds of jobs – Liverpool Football Club's proposals for the stadium are a key part of this. We are all committed to delivering a brighter future for Anfield and the club's exhibition is a clear signal that real progress is being made."

Liverpool City Council's planning committee had approved plans for phase one of the stadium redevelopment in September 2014. The expanded stand will comprise three tiers with the existing lower level reprofiled to accommodate a widened players' tunnel, new team benches, a media platform and wheelchair positions.

The Reds' owners were particularly pleased by the design after learning about ideas for the ultimately abandoned "hat-trick stand" that had been proposed for the Anfield Road end in the 1920s but which failed to advance beyond the planning stage. Sketches were also made for a triple-decker stand in the 1950s but these got no further than the architect's drawing board.

The new-look stand will include a specially designed colonnade for the Hillsborough Memorial and a new home for the Shankly Gates, as well as wider connections to Stanley Park and a space for fans to gather, thus enhancing the match day and non-match day experiences. Featuring the famous club crest, the structure will be visible from several points in the city and provide a striking addition to Liverpool's world-renowned skyline.

The club appointed construction company Carillion to rebuild the 21,000-capacity stand and hired Tom Doyle, the former project manager on the London 2012 Olympics plus the SSE Hydro Arena in Glasgow, to oversee the development.

Tom said: "One of the early challenges was keeping the stadium fully operational, with stadium tours and visits continuing all while we were building one of the largest all-seater stands in European football – it's a massive task but an amazing achievement which the club and its fans can be proud of when complete."

Careful testing was conducted into the stadium's acoustics and retaining the unique atmosphere was an important consideration throughout the planning stage.

Above: A view of the Anfield Road entrance to the Main Stand as it had looked since the installation of the Shankly Gates in August 1982. Shortly after this photograph was taken the gates were taken down and put in storage while the redevelopment work continues.

Opposite: The aspect changes in the spring of 2015 as the towering presence of the huge steel super-structure is put in place behind the existing Main Stand.

"Everyone at FSG is extremely proud and excited to be part of the expanding Anfield Stadium. Resolving the stadium issue will be our legacy at Liverpool."

Tom Werner, Liverpool Chairman

Tom added: "The legendary experience of Anfield makes the stadium one of the biggest attractions in the city and famous across the world. Protecting the special atmosphere has been a key consideration throughout the design process. The new Main Stand roof will direct the noise from Liverpool fans downwards and on to the pitch, protecting the unique atmosphere at Anfield."

Supporters attending matches during the second half of the 2014/15 season were able to witness the ongoing changes at each home game. The Hillsborough Memorial was removed to be placed in safe storage in January 2015 with the Shankly Gates following a month later. The first steel was assembled on site in March as work began on the super-structure behind the existing stand. Fans at the final home game of the season against Crystal Palace – Steven Gerrard's last match for the club in L4 – saw the huge steel framework in place behind the stand in readiness for the summer programme of works. This structure, constructed from 4,800 tonnes of steel, will eventually envelop the old stand and provide the two additional tiers.

With all the main foundations in place, work began on installing the stairs and metal decking that will hold the stand's new floor. Excavation work also commenced to complete the two huge tower bases that will support the steel roof truss.

Explaining the design, Tom Doyle said: "The enlarged structure will be 140 metres in length, 65 metres wide and up to 44 metres tall at its highest point, making it one of the largest single stands in Europe. The development will be constructed predominantly of two tonnes of red brick with a six- to eight-metre-high brick-clad podium running along the length of the stand with flights of steps at each end and a further flight in the centre.

"The podium will provide an active area, enclosed VIP parking and team coach drop-off and a natural segregation between lower and upper tier general admission access. The Hillsborough Memorial will be rehoused in a colonnade beneath the northern end of the podium. Two red-brick circulation cores will extend to the full height of the stand at either end while the central section will be glazed to provide views from the concourses and hospitality suites. The club's crest and Liver Bird will feature prominently on the fabric of the building. The new upper tier and main roof will have a splayed structure and gables and folded elements reducing the height and scale with existing adjoining stands.

"The design is innovative in terms of how it has met a challenging brief. One of the key tasks has been to design new large stands which are sympathetic to the existing stadium while maintaining the impression of it comprising four independent football stands. The stands have also been designed so that they can be constructed while maximizing use of the existing stands during the football season. The design will use materials that are sympathetic to the existing architecture and we will also retain the 1906 Archibald Leitch structure and will incorporate that into the expanded stand.

"We're also using modern methods of construction which meet the fast-track nature of the project. We've taken into consideration best practice for new and contemporary stadia. It will be safe, secure and inclusive and will be at the forefront of the Premier League in terms of variety and quality of fan experience. A further challenge was to contribute positively to the regeneration of the surrounding area, and it is our view that an expanded Anfield with a well-designed public realm achieves this."

Supporters have been able to keep track of progress via time-lapse footage available on the club's official website.

Once complete, Anfield will have around 7,000 hospitality seats, leaving Liverpool hopeful of being able to compete with rivals such as Arsenal and Chelsea in terms of match-day revenue. Figures from the 2012/13 season revealed Manchester United's match-day earnings were £109m, Arsenal's £93m, Chelsea's £71m and Liverpool's £45m, just ahead of Manchester City. A key element of this was corporate hospitality.

When the Reds had opened the Centenary Stand in 1992 the club were able to accommodate 30 glass-fronted executive boxes within it. But by 2010 Manchester United had 200 such boxes at Old Trafford while Arsenal included 150 at their 60,000-capacity Emirates Stadium.

Above: Specialist work has been conducted into the acoustics of the new-build to ensure the unique Anfield atmosphere is retained.

> ## "I'm delighted that the club are going for a traditional four-sided ground, keeping that distinctive, intimate element of Anfield, and that the architectural treatment of the new Main Stand will blend in with what's gone before."
>
> **Simon Inglis, author and football ground expert**

"Corporate hospitality revenues are essential," Ian Ayre told *FC Business* magazine in January 2015. "If we had increased capacity by 8,500 general admission seats only, it would have taken a ridiculous time to pay back the investment, meaning revenues into the team would have been affected. But the large corporate increase means we will pay the debt back quickly and not be saddled with debt, while quickly increasing revenues into the playing squad."

Players past and present, as well as commentators on stadium design, are enthused by the Reds' plans for 21st-century Anfield.

David Fairclough grew up in the area before going on to star in some of the Reds' most memorable nights of the 1970s. He says: "I spent the first 13 years of my life living about 100 yards away from Anfield. Our family home was on Carmel Street, between Beacon Lane and St Domingo Road. It was a great childhood and I have so many fond memories of the area. We would hang around outside Peter Thompson's garage – the site across the road from where the Twelfth Man pub is now – waiting to see him or some of the other players.

"But it was the football stadium that was the biggest part of my life. I was only about six or seven years old when my Dad – a season ticket holder – started taking me to reserve team games. Because the ground would be far from full I'd wander around with other kids. We'd go exploring the Main Stand or run up the steps of the Kop, which felt like climbing a mountain because we were so young. I have vivid recollections of walking all around the pitch and eventually ending up stood under the massive floodlight tower in the Annie Road end."

Fairclough, who scored one of the most famous goals at the stadium against St Etienne in 1977, believes the new designs for Anfield represent significant progress for the club.

He added: "Looking back, the stadium was fairly basic but that didn't matter. I don't think it ever crossed our minds. To us it meant absolutely everything. It really was the centre of my childhood. It is an iconic stadium and now it's going to be even better when the new stand is complete. The local community is a big part of any football club is. For me – as someone who hails from Anfield – it's crucial that the redevelopment goes hand in hand with regeneration. Everybody wins and surely that's the best result for the club, the people and the area."

Author and sports historian Simon Inglis has written a number of books on the subject of football stadiums and from what he's seen, he's impressed with the scheme. "What Liverpool Football Club have gone for is a tried and tested formula – building a new stand behind an existing one then linking them. It's an eminently sensible way to go, in my view a better solution than moving to Stanley Park. I'm delighted that the club are going for a traditional four-sided ground, keeping that distinctive, intimate element of Anfield, and that the architectural treatment of the new Main Stand will blend in with what's gone before.

"For me, the measure of the redevelopment's success will not only be how good a football experience it delivers – that should be a given with good design – but how it helps to transform the area around it, and thereby the perception of the football club as a positive presence. In that respect one of the scheme's most exciting elements is the opening up of the area behind the stand.

"And finally there is the whole notion of continuity: why start from scratch when you've got such a powerful asset in terms of heritage and international renown? You could describe it as a retro revival – a good old-fashioned, brand new redevelopment!"

From humble origins Anfield has developed into one of the most recognizable football grounds in the world and, although it's about to undergo another major change, an exciting new chapter in its fabled history will soon be written.

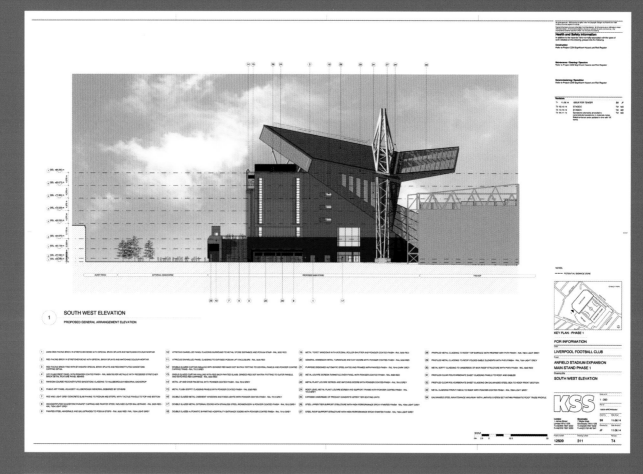

1 **SOUTH WEST ELEVATION**
PROPOSED GENERAL ARRANGEMENT ELEVATION

Health and Safety Information

KEY PLAN - PHASE 1

FOR INFORMATION

LIVERPOOL FOOTBALL CLUB

ANFIELD STADIUM EXPANSION
MAIN STAND PHASE 1

SOUTH WEST ELEVATION

KSS

12609   311   T4

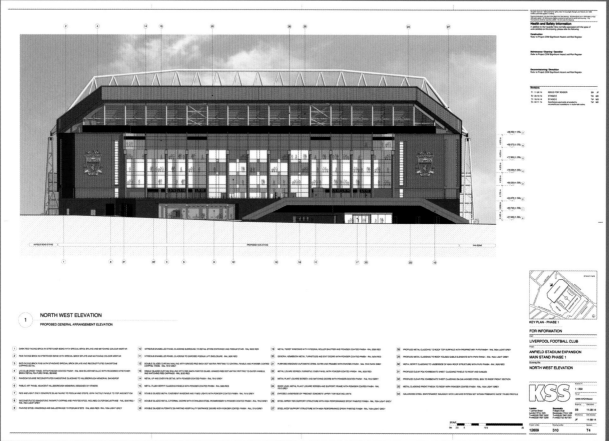

1 **NORTH WEST ELEVATION**
PROPOSED GENERAL ARRANGEMENT ELEVATION

Health and Safety Information

KEY PLAN - PHASE 1

FOR INFORMATION

LIVERPOOL FOOTBALL CLUB

ANFIELD STADIUM EXPANSION
MAIN STAND PHASE 1

NORTH WEST ELEVATION

KSS

12609   310   T4

"It is an iconic stadium and now it's going to be even better when the new stand is complete."

David Fairclough

Above: The new-look stand will feature tree-lined spaces behind it for fans to gather before Reds' fixtures and also on non-match days.

Opposite above: An image of how the new structure will look side-on as per the drawings produced by architects KSS.

Opposite below: The architects' North-West elevation sketch of the imposing new-look Main Stand, which will feature the Reds' famous club crest at either end.

"The new Main Stand roof will direct the noise from Liverpool fans downwards and onto the pitch, protecting the unique atmosphere at Anfield."

Tom Doyle, Anfield development manager

Right: The back-lit stadium will be one of the most imposing in Liverpool once daylight falls and will be visible from various parts of the city.

Following pages: The new-look Anfield promises to be an incredible arena, particularly when the Reds stage more of those European nights under the lights.

A TIMELINE OF ANFIELD'S SIGNIFICANT CHANGES, MOMENTS AND GAMES...

1884
- Everton Football Club move into Anfield Road and a crowd of 1,000 watch the first ever game against Earlestown

1885
- A then record Anfield crowd of 3,500 watch Everton take on FA Cup holders Blackburn Rovers

1886
- Work is completed on the first ever stand at the south side of the ground, what we now know as the Kop

1887
- Anfield's first ever 10,000 crowd watch Everton play Preston

1888
- FA Cup semi-final: Preston North End 5-0 Crewe Alexandra
- Anfield hosts its first Football League game as Everton beat Accrington

1897
- The Anfield Road end of the ground is covered with a roof

1903
- The first Anfield Road terrace is built

1905
- International: England 3-1 Wales (British Championship)

1906
- Archibald Leitch is commissioned to redevelop Anfield. The changes include the resiting of the Main Stand and the construction of a large uncovered terrace that became the Kop

1908
- FA Cup semi-final: Newcastle United 6-0 Fulham

1912
- FA Cup semi-final: Blackburn Rovers 0-0 West Bromwich Albion

1929
- FA Cup semi-final: Bolton Wanderers 3-1 Huddersfield Town

1931
- International: England 3-1 Wales (British Championship)

1932
- A new attendance record of 57,804 is set when Chelsea come to Anfield for a FA Cup quarter-final

1934
- Anfield accommodates its first 60,000-plus crowd as Liverpool and Tranmere Rovers meet in a FA Cup 4th-round tie

1937
- The legendary Fred Perry is the star attraction in an exhibition tennis tournament at Anfield

1963
- A cantilever stand is built on the Kemlyn Road

1964
- Liverpool are champions
- Anfield stages its first game in European competition
- *Match of the Day*'s first ever programme is broadcast from Anfield

1965
- The Anfield Road end is rebuilt with a new roof

1966
- Liverpool beat Chelsea 2-1 at Anfield to clinch a seventh League title

1967
- A FA Cup tie versus Everton at Goodison is relayed on giant screens at Anfield

1978
- The Boys' Pen is closed

1979
- Aston Villa are defeated 3-0 as another league title is celebrated

1980
- Liverpool are crowned champions for an 12th time following a 4-1 home win over Aston Villa on the final Saturday of the league season
- The paddock is seated

1982
- Liverpool secure the League Championship and supporters stand on the Anfield Road terraces for a final time
- The Shankly Gates are erected in memory of the great manager

1984
- Anfield hosts a series of sermons by American evangelist Billy Graham

1987
- A collapsed sewer under the Kop forces Liverpool to postpone their first three home games of the season

1994
- To comply with the Taylor Report the Spion Kop terrace is demolished and a new grandstand constructed transforming Anfield into an all-seater stadium

1995
- International: Republic of Ireland 0-2 Holland (Euro 96 play-off)

1996
- Anfield plays host to the four games in Euro 96: Italy 2-1 Russia;; Czech Republic 2-1 Italy; Russia 3-3 Czech Republic; France 0-0 Holland

1997
- An upper tier is added to the Anfield Road stand

1998
- International: Wales 0-2 Italy (Euro 2000 qualifier)

1999
- The Paisley Gateway is erected outside the Kop in honour of the club's most successful ever manager
- International: Wales 0-2 Denmark (Euro 2000 qualifier)

Far left: A Liverpool goal against Aston Villa in 1980 brings delight to fans and players.

Left: Same place, different time: Anfield erupts once again as the modern-day team congratulate each other after hitting the back of those red nets.

1889
- International: England 6-1 Ireland (British Championship)

1890
- Everton trial the use of floodlights at Anfield

1891
- Anfield celebrates its first league title as Everton are crowned champions
- A flagpole from the ship SS *Great Eastern* is put in place at Anfield

1892
- Everton leave Anfield following a dispute over rent, leading to the formation of Liverpool Football Club

1894
- A new Anfield attendance record is set as 18,000 witness a memorable FA Cup victory over Preston
- Liverpool's first Main Stand is built, holding 3,000

1920
- The first 50,000 crowd is recorded at Anfield

1921
- The King and Queen attend the FA Cup semi-final between Wolves and Cardiff

1922
- A rare goal by winger Fred Hopkin is greeted by the outbreak of a fire at the Anfield Road end

1922
- The Boys' Pen is opened at the Anfield Road end of the Kemlyn Road paddock
- International: England 3-1 Wales (British Championship)

1926
- International: England 3-3 Ireland (British Championship)

1928
- A roof is put on the Kop

1947
- The Boys' Pen is moved from the Kemlyn Road to the Kop

1952
- Anfield's all-time record attendance of 61,905 is set when Wolves visit for an FA Cup fourth-round tie

1957
- Floodlights are installed and switched on for the first time in a 3-2 victory over Everton

1958
- The world-famous Harlem Globetrotters basketball team play an exhibition game in front of the Kop

1962
- Liverpool secure promotion back to the top flight after a 2-0 win over Southampton at Anfield

1971
- The TV gantry in the Main Stand is used for the first time when Liverpool play Bayern Munich in the quarter-final of the European Cup Winners' Cup

1973
- A redeveloped Main Stand is officially opened
- Anfield's highest average attendance of 48,103 is recorded

1974
- The now famous "This Is Anfield" sign is put up in the players' tunnel

1976
- Anfield's record European attendance of 55,104 is set against Barcelona in the UEFA Cup semi-final second leg

1977
- International: Wales 0-2 Scotland (World Cup qualifier)

1988
- Liverpool are crowned champions for a 17th time following a 1-0 victory over Tottenham at Anfield

1989
- Anfield becomes a shrine to victims of the Hillsborough disaster and fences are removed from the front of the Kop

1990
- The Hillsborough Memorial is unveiled
- Anfield hails Liverpool's 18th League Championship success following victory over Queens Park Rangers

1991
- Penrith Panthers beat Wigan Warriors to claim the World Club Rugby League Challenge

1992
- To commemorate the club's centenary year an upper tier is added to the Kemlyn Road stand, which is renamed the Centenary Stand

2001
- International: England 2-1 Finland (World Cup qualifier)

2002
- Plans are revealed for a new 55,000-seater stadium in Stanley Park
- International: England 4-0 Paraguay (Friendly)

2006
- International: England 2-1 Uruguay (Friendly)

2008
- To celebrate Liverpool's Capital of Culture status Anfield hosts a concert featuring Paul McCartney

2014
- It's announced that Liverpool will not be leaving Anfield and plans are unveiled for the redevelopment of the Main Stand

INDEX

CREDITS

The publishers would like to thank the following sources for their kind permission to reproduce the pictures in this book.

Imagery © Liverpool Football Club & Athletic Grounds Ltd. with the following exceptions:

Corbis: /Colorsport: 44-45

Getty Images: /Vincent Amalvy/AFP: 162B; /Clive Brunskill: 96-97; /Central Press/Hulton Archive: 123BL; /MJ Kim/MPL Communications Ltd: 168T; Popperfoto: 19; /Bob Thomas/Popperfoto: 14; /William Vanderson/Picture Post: 73B

Adrian Killen: 70-71T, 131T

Press Association Images: /Matthew Ashton: 162T; /David Kendall: 165B

Private Collection: 52, 56, 71B

Gary Shaw: 66

Wikimedia Commons: 42

Every effort has been made to acknowledge correctly and contact the source and/or copyright holder of each picture and Carlton Books Limited apologizes for any unintentional errors or omissions that will be corrected in future editions of this book.

ACKNOWLEDGMENTS

In no particular order the authors would like to thank the following for their help in the production of this book Kjell Hanssen (kjellhanssen.com), Adrian Killen, Stephen Done, Alan Herr, John Williams, Steve Horton, Jonny Stokkeland, Arnie Baldursson (lfchistory.net), Gary Shaw, David Cottrell, Vicky Ndukwe, Christina Kilkenny and Paul Owen.

"I can remember the floodlights dazzling my eyes because it was a night game, and the green colour of the pitch. It looked amazing and gave me such a buzz."

Steven Gerrard on his very first visit to Anfield

Below: The sanctuary of the home dressing room at Anfield, ready and waiting for the arrival of the players prior to a crucial game during the spring of 2014.